A Concise History
of
PREACHING

D0027029

Preachers and teachers of preaching have been profiting recently by reading current approaches to biblical study and current theories of literary criticism. This reading has been most helpful and most refreshing for the field of preaching.

Paul Wilson has now rendered us a great service by reminding us that there is yet another field of great nourishment for us, and that is the history of our own discipline. Paul has in this brief work not only put us again in fruitful touch with our own history and our own esteemed predecessors, but he has teased us into more active thought.

—Fred B. Craddock
Professor of Preaching and New Testament,
Candler School of Theology, Emory University

This is a welcome book; it has a human touch. The writer makes the lives and emphases of twenty selected preachers accessible and interesting. This book will help the church affirm and nourish its history and its potential.

—Barbara Bate
Director of Preaching Ministries,
Section on Worship, The United Methodist Church

Inspirational and instructive, dealing with names as familiar as Luther or exotic as Romanos the Melodist, [Wilson's book] can help us all in our solemn common task.

—O. C. Edwards
Professor of Preaching,
Seabury-Western Theological Seminary

A Concise History
of
PREACHING

Paul Scott Wilson

ABINGDON PRESS
Nashville

A CONCISE HISTORY OF PREACHING

Copyright © 1992 by Abingdon Press

This book is printed on acid-free, recycled paper.

Library of Congress Cataloging-in-Publication Data

Wilson, Paul Scott, 1949-
    A concise history of preaching / Paul Scott Wilson.
        p.   cm.
    Includes bibliographical references.
    ISBN 0-687-09342-2 (pbk. : alk. paper)
    1. Preaching—History. I. Title.
    BV4207.W53   1992   92-16294
    251'.009—dc20   CIP

Grateful acknowledgment is made for the use of excerpts from the following:

From the New Revised Standard Version Bible, copyright © 1989, by the Division of Christian Education of the National Council of the Churches of Christ in the United States of America. Used by permission.

From the Revised Standard Version of the Bible, copyright 1946, 1952, 1971 by the Division of Christian Education of the National Council of Churches of Christ in the U.S.A. Used by permission.

From the King James or Authorized Version of the Bible.

The quotation from John Donne on p. 7 is from "Problem XV: Why Puritans make long Sermons?" in John Donne, *Paradoxes and Problems,* ed. Helen Peters (Oxford: Clarendon Press, 1980), pp. 43-44. Used by permission of Oxford University Press.

Cover: The Preaching Scene in a Churchyard. An engraving from *Ms. Fitzwilliam Mus., Cambridge, 22, p. 55.*

ACKNOWLEDGMENTS

An expression of deep gratitude is owed a number of people who have assisted in various ways in this project, and who bear no responsibility for its shortcomings: to my students; to my colleagues Phyllis D. Airhart, Gordon Harland, Gerald Hobbs, Thomas G. Long, Ian Manson, Charles L. Rice, Leif Vaage, Robert Waznak; to Principal John C. Hoffman of Emmanuel College and to the Board of Regents of Victoria University; to the Academy of Homiletics; to Paul Franklyn and Steven W. Cox at Abingdon Press; and not least, to my family.

To Deanna, my beloved friend,
companion, lover, minister, and wife.

Problem:
Why Puritans
make long sermons?

*I*t needes not for perspicuousnesse, For
God knowes they are playne enough. Nor doe all of them
use the long Sembriefe Accent, some of them have Cro-
chets enough. It may bee they pretend not to rise like glorious Tapers or Torches, but like long thinne wretched and
sick watch candles, which languish and are in a dimme
consumption from the first Minute, yet spend more tyme
in theyr glimmeringe, yea in theyr snuff and stinke, then
others in theyr more profitable glory. I have thought sometimes that out of conscience they allow large measure to
course ware, And sometimes that usurping in that place a
liberty to speake freely of Kings and all, they think themselves Kings then and would raigne as long as they could.
But now I thinke they doe it out of a Zealous Imagination
that it is theyr duty to preache on till theyr Auditory wake
agayne.

—John Donne

CONTENTS

Contents

INTRODUCTION

This modest introductory volume to the history of Christian preaching is written for preachers, students, and teachers who are interested in learning more about preaching for today from perhaps a surprising source, given the need for relevance—from great preachers and traditions of the past. This is something of an excursion tour, stopping for visits with twenty preachers, who will provide important homiletical insights. We will walk with them through their hometowns, chat with them as they prepare to preach, overhear portions of their sermons, and then reflect about what we might learn. The purpose here is largely homiletical, to stimulate the creativity of the preacher today.

The purpose here is also historical, although I hasten to add that I am not a historian. Those who legitimately call themselves historians have their own canons of materials, which they use according to their own methodologies and ends. Traditionally they have shown reluctance to use sermons, perhaps because they are unsure how to use them. Even as I lift up some of what is important from a homiletical perspective, I seek forgiveness from those who have steeped their lives in history who may find I am wearing coarse boots where I should be treading barefoot.

There are many ways to write history. One can trace the

development of great ideas. One can follow great social, economic, political, religious, and cultural movements. One can focus on the lives of significant individuals; or on those people who are marginalized by the recorded materials; or on particular kinds of historical data—archeological evidence, literary sources or documents. The approach here is shaped by methodological concerns from the discipline of homiletics. It combines a biographical history that pays particular attention to preaching, with a history of ideas. As is appropriate to a homiletical text, ideas receiving attention here have to do with homiletical-rhetorical method; form and content; hermeneutics and the history of interpretation theory; theology, both as it understands the act of proclamation and as it shapes the content; and pastoral care.

Another purpose is to provide a history that is concise. The difficulty of choosing only a few persons from history is not much diminished if instead of choosing twenty, that number is doubled, or even tripled. Any such study is unavoidably limited not least by the person making the choices and by principles of selection. With the thousands of choices available, no two persons are apt to make the same selections. This is simply to recognize the limitations of this project from the start. But there can be advantages to this approach as well, an approach that might be characterized as case study, focusing on particular moments with as much fullness as possible. Here we will begin to get a clear sense of some individual preachers and point beyond these to historical themes. An alternative and complementary approach to the broad history of preaching is to survey historical themes and point to individuals, as Yngve Brilioth was the last to do, perhaps failing to give a sufficient sense of any one preacher.[1] Like any excursion tour, this one must try to be representative, not comprehensive. We will be flying past the territory of many preachers and landing to speak to a few.

A final purpose of these pages is to stimulate excitement and interest in the vast horizons of preaching we may glimpse through the windows this study provides. Three periods are identified, the Early Church and the Middle Ages being the first two. The third, from Luther and the printing press up to modern times, is of such continuing diversity and pluralism that it is designated here simply as the period of reformations. Our tour ends in 1968 with the death of Martin Luther King, Jr., and the retirement of James S. Stewart.

There are many lines of emphasis we could follow through these periods. The one chosen here is "authority." From the beginning of the church, authority has been an issue: By what right does anyone preach, teach, or claim one interpretation of Scripture to be superior to another? Even in the Middle Ages, when Scripture was the relatively private text of a small educated elite and church control might be said to have been at its peak, the rumblings of challenge were never silenced. When central ecclesial authority was radically overthrown by the Protestants in their Reformation, the foundations of other challenges to subsequent authorities were simultaneously and unavoidably laid. As history has taught us many times, the overthrow of central authority spawns multiple competing claims. The issue of authority is heightened in Protestant circles by the central emphasis, not on the eucharist, but on the interpretation of the Word.

Studies in the history of preaching, of which there have been few this century, tend to ignore evidence about the preaching of the infant church because no hardened sermonic form can be identified there; thus, the true beginning is often considered to be with Origen two centuries later. The picture is further muddied by our tendency to project back into history definitions of preaching more rigid than are appropriate for the times. Thus our studies also result in a history of great men, or a history of the ordained, or a history of pulpit preachers, to the exclusion of many. In the confined space here, some encouragement is given in a small way to begin correcting these deficiencies.

For example, historian Giorgio Otranto, director of the Institute for Classical and Christian Studies at the University of Bari, Italy, on a recent North American lecture tour provided evidence that until the fourth century women held the role of priests. His photographs of newly excavated or archeological sites include: a fresco on the walls of the Priscilla Catacomb in Rome depicting women blessing the eucharistic bread; tomb inscriptions from Italy and France identifying women named Leta, Flavia, Maria, and Marta as priests; and from the Church of St. Praxidus in Rome a mosaic of four bishops including one woman, Theodora.[2] St. Geneviève (429–511), patron saint of Paris, was an active preacher until a canon in 475 forbade women from preaching in public as being offensive to men. She functioned as the nontitular bishop of Paris.[3] Even after their prohibition as priests, women continued to preach in a variety of formal and informal capacities through history. Actual documents of sermons are scarce, although some of the documents we do have, particularly from medieval abbesses, await to be claimed as sermons. In this present study three women are included, one in each of our time periods.

Thousands of preachers from around the world await rediscovery in their sermons, books, and archival papers. A forthcoming lengthy study from O. C. Edwards will contribute greatly to our knowledge.[4] The vastness of untapped resources suggests that the history of preaching will be an area of increasing importance for various disciplines in the next decades. We can never truly speak of a broad history of Christian preaching until such a time as we have (1) various cultural, regional, national, and global perspectives on the subject, including the history of missions; (2) the important histories of preaching in the Roman Catholic and Orthodox traditions; and (3) studies of preaching in the other great faith traditions.

With the exceptions of the Roman Catholic preaching Orders, two of which are discussed here, and of many individual excellent preachers who could have been included here had there been space, it has been Protestants who have placed most emphasis on preaching, making it the center of their worship. The preachers chosen for the post-Reformation period are primarily Protestant. They were selected partly to provide samples from various denominations. Although limited to North America, Great Britain, and to a lesser extent continental Europe, perhaps this small collection of subjects will serve, at minimum, as an invitation and encouragement to readers to make their own further explorations of the preaching of yesterday—and today.

I.
THE EARLY CHURCH

The Authority of
the Word as Sound

To speak of the inherent authority of "the word as sound" in the early church is to remind ourselves that the ways we think of a "word" or the "Word" are radically different from ancient ways. When we think of a word, we think of letters on a page. When we think of God's Word, our first association is with the Bible, a sacred written text. When we meditate further, of course, we come to a truer understanding of word as the living Word, as event, as Christ in our midst. This latter understanding is much closer to the ancient thinking about words in general. The Hebrew term for "word" is *dabar*, which means "event" in many contexts. Isaiah told us that "the Word of God goes forth and it does not return empty or void." Blessings that are uttered cannot be revoked. Some of our most intriguing theological ideas (such as Word as event) originally stem from oral ways of thinking. They exist on the plains of modern lettered thought like intriguing glacial remnants of an age now receded, when oral ways of thinking were dominant.

The scriptures were written by people similar in some ways to us, well-versed in language and writing. But unlike us, their ways of thinking and ordering thought were shaped at deep, primitive, and pervasive levels by the highly sophisticated oral, largely unlettered culture that surrounded them in their world. Their understanding of the idea of word came from the way they read. Reading was out loud; it was not done silently. That is the reason Philip, in the book of Acts, knew the Ethiopian eunuch was reading Isaiah before joining him in his chariot (8:27). That is also a reason Origen made a distinction between a "carnal," "corporeal," or "literal" meaning of a text (i.e., the meaning received from the simple physical hearing of a text read aloud), and a "spiritual" meaning (i.e., the text fully understood and appropriated in one's life).

When Augustine went to visit Ambrose in his study, he expected to overhear him reading and was shocked, amazed, and rudely disappointed that no sound was uttered. For him it was not a matter of choice whether one read silently or aloud: Reading and sound went together. In ancient culture those who had mastered the high technology of script were the receivers of inaudible sounds recorded on the page that were then amplified and transmitted to the community. Those who were interested listeners would gather around readers to hear voices from distant places, much as our great grandparents gathered around the first community radios, or as we gather around television.

A word for ancient people was not in the first instance a marking on a page, the way it is for us. Rather it was a sound that was uttered (= outered), and the marking on the page prompted the correct sound. It was the aural or acoustic image heard by the ear that stimulated the mental idea, not the visual image on the page. In sounding a word, in breathing it, one understood its meaning. As Paul said, "The letter kills, but the Spirit gives life" (II Cor. 3:6). Moreover, there was power inherent in the sounded word, as witnessed by the ancient scriptural understandings of the power of a name and, at a more basic level, by God's act of creation through speaking.

The aurality of the Word is relevant to the history of preaching. First, the ancient Scriptures primarily existed as sound, even after they were written. In the first-century synagogue, the distinction between reading and interpretation of Scripture was made partly on the basis of volume of sound: To honor the text the interpreter could not speak louder than the reader.[1] In the infant church the distinctions are vague: the lines dividing reading, witnessing, and preaching are not so distinct as we would make them, nor were those distinctions an interest of an oral culture.

Second, ancient oral culture is partially accessible to us through ancient rules of rhetoric, rules for effective oral discourse and argumentation. Although they exist as written rules to be followed in the proper ordering of sound and thought, they were primarily a reflection of oral principles that already lay embedded in the culture all around them, undergirding good speech. By Jesus' time classical rhetoric formed the foundation of formal education in the Hellenistic and Roman world.

Third, as long as words exist in the first instance as sounds "out there," rather than on a page as images adjacent to other surrounding images, there is greater freedom for interpretation. They exist more on their own, less bound by their context. Simply the word *context* (= with text) implies a written text, a lettered way of thought. This understanding of the relative independence of scriptural words we will experience repeatedly in the approaches to preaching in the early church and beyond.

Fourth, the early church does not know history as we know it. The past is of less interest in itself than in its connection to the present and future. Scripture is less a written history than it is the sound of God's voice speaking right now to the present. This is best captured in the words of Justin Martyr as he writes to the Romans and Greeks concerning the prophets:

When you hear the words of prophets spoken as in a particular character, do not think them as spoken by the inspired men themselves, but by the divine Word that moved them. For sometimes he speaks as predicting the things that are to happen, sometimes he speaks as in the character of God the Master and Father of all, sometimes as in the character of Christ, sometimes in the character of the people answering the Lord or his Father. You can see the same thing in your own writers, where one man is the author of the whole work but introduces different characters in dialogue.[2]

When we come to Chrysostom and the school of Antioch, which is based on what many call a historical approach to Scripture, we will see that this history is still based more in sound than is linear history, which is, after all, much more recent. It springs in part from the linear ways in which we write script, if we accept Walter J. Ong's thesis.[3] With Augustine we will see in the West the beginning of an important shift away from sound and toward the page. These gradual shifts will start a landslide in Luther's day with the printing press. But it will take hundreds of years for the sound of the page to die away.

THE PROCLAIMED WORD TAKING SHAPE

CHAPTER 1

The Pre-gospels and Paul
The New Testament as Preaching

If the intent here were to provide a comprehensive history of preaching we would start with both the Old Testament and the history of rhetoric, and move to the preaching of John the Baptist and Jesus as recorded in the Gospels, the preaching of the women as the first proclaimers of the resurrection, and the preaching of Paul and Peter, as recorded in Acts. But given our concise scope, we begin our tour by claiming that the book we call the New Testament originates in the preaching of the infant church.

The Pre-gospel Preaching

A gap of maybe thirty years appears after the death and resurrection of Jesus before any written record of him was made. What was going on in that time? What he said and did was not lost. Rather it was kept alive orally by wandering charismatic healer-preachers[1] and by the followers of Christ, who would gather to celebrate the resurrection, to pray, to partake in the Lord's Supper, to read "the writings" (i.e., Scripture), and to retell what they remembered of Jesus' ministry and teachings. They told their stories of Christ for a variety of reasons, including: (1) as a witness to the Good News of Christ; (2) to win followers of Christ; (3) in order that details not be forgotten; (4) because the stories and sayings of Christ made sense of their continuing experience of him; (5) to shape their own community life such that their lives would be a witness to the truth of Christ; (6) to help settle disputes, for instance with the followers of John the Baptist; (7) as a part of their searching the Scriptures for clues to the meaning of Christ; (8) as a form of oral commentary on the Scriptures; and (9) eventually as a way of understanding their increasing ostracism from the synagogues. For these charismatic itinerants, unlike Paul's communities, the preaching centered on the stories and sayings of Jesus.

The preaching of the infant church that later formed the Gospels remained in oral form because of community focus on spiritual discipline and the expectation of Christ's immanent return. Another important reason was the prohibition against writing. Already at the time of Jesus there were two massive and unwritten movements underway. One would eventually result in the written text of the Mishnah, a Hebrew commentary on the Jewish Law, and the other would result in the Targum, a translation of the Scriptures into Aramaic, the common language of the day. Both of these oral projects were committed to memory, for to use writing was to place them on an equal footing with "That Which Was Written." (Scholars in Jerusalem were regretting this had already happened, three centuries earlier, in Alexandria with the translation of the Torah into the Greek Septuagint.) It was many years before this prohibition against writing was dropped.[2] In time, the writing of the oral accounts of Jesus, within the Jewish ethos in particular, was acknowledgment of the divine status and authority given to Jesus' words and acts. The written texts were also of assistance in remembering the stories and sayings, and in further moving the witness of the Jesus tradition out of the Aramaic-speaking world and into the Greek.

The pre-gospel preaching tends to center on stories and sayings and to avoid convoluted argumentation. Jewish exegesis of the day interpreted the Law using principles that included: arguing from the simple to the difficult, or the lesser to the greater; applying one or more laws; use of analogy; and moving from the general to the particular or vice versa. The early Christians employed these methods. Scripture is used as prophecy of Christ, as proof text, and as that which underlines the uniqueness of his message. Preachers found in Jesus' words hints of events taking place in their own times, such as the rejection of Jesus' teachings, their own persecutions, and their expectation of his immediate return. They found ways of interpreting and reassessing Scripture that, for them, arrived at the heart of the Jewish faith. They made little distinction between what Jesus said during his ministry and what he was currently saying to them.

The Preaching of Paul

Throughout his missionary activity Paul preached to both Jew and Gentile that Jesus was the fulfillment of the promises to Israel. Paul would proclaim God's word in the synagogue, in the Christian gatherings, and presumably in the market squares as he joined the tentmakers. After he left a community (though in the case of Romans it was before he arrived), he wrote to them as a way of continuing to exercise his God-given authority among them. New Testament scholars, uninvolved in rhetorical criticism, tend to speak of the letters as essays, because we are not sure what sermons looked like. It may be more sensible not to expect a single form. The sermon was still taking shape. Here we assert that Paul's letters are sermons, although there are a variety of ways in which this designation should be qualified.

Letters were typically brief and sent with a messenger, who regularly carried orally the most important elements of the communication. Paul's letters are unique in antiquity, partly because of their length. Some of his possible messengers are named, including Timothy in I Corinthians 4:17 and possibly Phoebe, a coworker, in Romans 16:1. The letters are intended to be read when the congregation is gathered (i.e., I Thess. 5:27; II Thess. 3:14; Philem. 2*b*). Custom suggests that the bearers of his letters were sent with his authority to interpret and expand points that might be unclear.

The sermonic possibilities of his letters extend beyond the oral nature of their delivery. Apart from the opening and closing sections, almost no parallels have been found in other letters of the time. If we are looking at Christian sermons, not letters or essays, the possibilities (excluding Philemon) could be: (1) single sermons intended to be delivered at their destination or already delivered in some form elsewhere; (2) multiple sermons—I and II Corinthians, Romans, and Philippians in particular show the hand of a redactor; (3) sermons recorded by a secretary—the dialogical style Paul often uses may reflect actual conversations that took place; (4) sermons sent in a form that mirrors the actions of the gathered community, together with the opening greetings in the name of Christ, various liturgical suggestions (including greeting one another with the holy kiss), and concluding benedictions.

In sending his spoken word to the communities, he claims the same authority as if he were actually present. As he says, "For though absent in body, I am present in spirit. . . . When you are assembled, and my spirit is present with the power of our Lord Jesus, you are to hand this man over to Satan" (I Cor. 5:3-5). Paul wants his message delivered in the setting of worship to remind his people that he is still preaching, still presiding, still in charge under Christ, still very much with them even if at a distance.

If we understand Paul's letters in various ways as his sermons we discover a number of things. Foremost among these is that Paul's preaching differs radically from the pre-gospel preaching of his contemporaries in the Jerusalem-centered church. It is primarily centered in conceptual argument, not narratives which dominate the Jesus traditions. If Paul knows any stories of the life and ministry of Christ, apart from the institutional narrative, the crucifixion and resurrection, he makes no use of them. He uses Scripture with great frequency, though not in detailed fashion. He often appeals to texts as simple proofs of arguments (what we call today "prooftexting") and will follow a brief explanation of a text with an application. He sees Adam as a "type" of Christ (Rom. 5:14). He finds in Hagar and Sarah an "allegory" concerning the two covenants (Gal. 4:24). His uses of Scripture, particularly of types and allegory, will be expanded and developed by later preachers, largely due to his precedent. What we see in Paul and the pre-gospels is the proclaimed word still taking shape.

Invention or the discovery of possible arguments tended to be the primary focus of ancient rhetoric. The arrangement and style of speeches was a secondary focus. The usual pattern included an **introduction** *(exordium)*; a **narration** or summary of the relevant events *(narratio)* including a clear statement of the issue, basic facts, the thesis and one's rationale; the **argument** *(confirmatio)* or proof divided into parts, which was the main body of the speech and included arguments for and against one's position; and a **conclusion** *(conclusio)*. Some observers have found these patterns in both modes of early Christian preaching.

Sermon Sample

Rhetoric, broadly conceived as "established oral ways of persuasive speech," is fundamental to all early church preaching. Burton L. Mack provides analyses of excerpts from the Synoptic Gospels and Paul, including the following from I Corinthians 15:1-58. Mack calls it a "perfect" example of rhetorical argument. It might represent a full homily, if we could apply today's values to Paul's thought.

Thesis: There Will Be a Resurrection

Exordium

[introduction]:	Address to the Corinthians with reminder of their reception of the gospel (vv. 1-2)

Narratio

[statement of the case]:	How the preaching of the kerygma, including the resurrection of Christ, came to the Corinthians (vv. 3-11)
Issue:	Some say that there is no resurrection of the dead. (vv. 12-19)
Fact:	In fact Christ was raised from the dead.
Thesis:	The first fruits of those who have died (v. 20)

Argument

[including here a division of the points, a proof of the case, and a refutation of the opposing arguments]:

Paradigms:	Just as Adam brought death, so Christ brought life. (vv. 21-28)
Opposite:	Each in his own order
Examples:	Baptizing for the dead
	Dying daily for the gospel
	Fighting beasts at Ephesus (vv. 29-34)
Analogies:	Seed that dies and comes to life
	Different kinds of body (vv. 35-44)

| Citation: | The Genesis account of the creation of Adam, a "living being," from the dust (vv. 45-50) |
| **Conclusion:** | A narrative description of the eschatological resurrection of the dead, a scriptural citation, a thanksgiving, and an exhortation (vv. 51-58)[3] |

Within this argument, Mack notes the following "interlocking chain":

> If Christ is not raised, then preaching is in vain.
> If preaching is vain, then your faith is vain.
> If faith is vain, then you are yet in your sins.
> If sin is still victor, then the dead have perished.
> If that is the case, then we are to be pitied.

This is Mack's rhetorical analysis of the narrative in Mark 10:17-31:

Thesis: How to Inherit Eternal Life

Narrative:	A righteous man with great possessions asks about inheriting eternal life. (vv. 17-22)
Issue:	What one should do (v. 17)
Thesis:	One should sell possessions, give to the poor, and follow Jesus. (v. 21)
Reason:	One will have treasure in heaven. (v. 21)
Argument:	
From the Opposite:	
Paradigm:	The man went away sorrowful. (v. 22)
Analogy:	It is easier for a camel to pass through the eye of a needle, than for the wealthy to enter the kingdom of God. (vv. 23-25)
Issue:	Then who can be saved? (v. 26)

For the Thesis:	With God it is possible. (v. 27)
Paradigm:	The disciples have left everything to follow Jesus. (v. 28)
Analogy:	Receiving a hundredfold reward (vv. 29-30)
Conclusion:	
Maxim:	The first will be last, and the last first. (v. 31)[4]

Implications

To describe what we may learn from the preaching of the infant church is to explain what we might learn from what is now New Testament Scripture. On occasion we should try for ourselves some of the rhetorical devices we find in the texts; devices such as (1) the interlocking chain or (2) the "mystic ladder" found for instance in Romans 5:3ff. and 8:29ff.

Tom Long suggests that we imitate the form and function of the biblical text in our particular sermon.[5] Raymond Bailey's suggestions pick up on the importance of the oral thought patterns in the texts: Write for the ear not the eye; use the active voice and vivid verbs that describe or call for actions; use language that has emotional and sensory appeal; speak of the self; and identify personal benefits of the faith.[6]

There is a further possibility. When we arrive at Aquinas we will see that the only records of his sermons are highly condensed outlines that were intended to be expanded by himself as he preached and by his students as they went out to preach. What would a sermon on Paul or the Gospels be like if we similarly took the texts' rhetorical divisions, as we might interpret them, one at a time, as the basis for our expansion and proclamation of the text?

We might also try some of the important suggestions for discovering something to say. For example, we might use the Hebrew pattern of arguing from the simple to the difficult, or the lesser to the greater, or the particular to the general, or vice versa. Or we might try the Markan approach, mentioned earlier, of arguing first from the opposite of the thesis (no eternal life) and then for the thesis (it is possible); or from a paradigm (Adam) to an analogy (seed) to an issue (resurrection). Both propositional and narrative sermons can have these components, as the preacher creates a spark between opposite poles.[7]

There is a theological learning that is perhaps more important than anything else, however. For the infant church the proclaimed Word brings an end to the old world and brings in the new. It is here, in the preaching and the sacraments, that the salvation event takes place. When we preach, we set in motion God's purposes for the world. As we preach, God's love takes shape in the present. In speaking, the Word once again becomes flesh as it starts to be enacted in our lives. The world we dream as possible through our faith is the world that God wills for all, and it has as its place of in-breaking the sermons we preach. It is not that if we fail to dream it, it will not happen; it is that if we dream it, it will start to happen. Isaiah's assertion that God's Word "does not return empty or void" can be our constant understanding. It is for this reason that we can and should be both bold and daring in discerning, imagining, and picturing God's will in detail. Preaching is an earth-shaking event! We need be no less hesitant about claiming God's presence in our sounded words than were the first preachers.

CHAPTER 2

Perpetua (c. 181–203)
Martyrdom as the Highest Form of Witness

Perpetua was a young nursing mother of exuberant faith who died as a martyr. She was from a wealthy family in the port city of Carthage, Northwest Africa, and was only twenty-two when arrested along with her brother, other Christian friends, and Felicitas, her young pregnant servant. We know nothing of her husband; she commends her son into her parents' care before her death.

Martyrdom was not something new to Carthage. Around the time of Perpetua's birth, some humble people from a neighboring town were executed for refusing to forswear their Christianity. To convert to a foreign cult not formally recognized by the state, such as Christianity, was disdained by the educated elite as much as it was mistrusted. Charges of atheism could lead to trial. The state, for its part, was generally less interested in killing Christians than it was in unifying a divisive empire and preventing civil strife.

Perpetua would have heard sermons praising martyrs who were rewarded for their sacrifice with full pardon of all sins and union with Christ. She would have received encouragement in her confirmation classes not to deny the Holy Spirit (Mark 3:29). And she had already adopted a defiance of the world that characterized the charismatic

North African church. At the time she was arrested she had not yet been baptized. At her baptism a few days later, while still under arrest, she embraced her suffering as union with Christ, but she lamented the physical, social, and emotional suffering caused to her parents and family. She and Felicitas were to be killed by a mad heifer (instead of a bull, in deference to their gender), but having survived, they were eventually put to death by the sword on either March 2 or 7, 203.

Perpetua's moving autobiographical story was circulated widely and eventually used in the formal liturgy of the church. She was recognized both as a prophetess and as a woman of remarkable courage in the face of persecution. The basilica at Carthage was dedicated to her, and the anniversary of her martyrdom was recognized in the Roman calendar.

Homiletical Setting

A history of preaching needs to include mention of the early Christian martyrs. Perpetua's account is the earliest known Christian writing by a woman, one of the earliest reliable autobiographical accounts of imprisonment and trial for martyrdom, and is the model for later martyrdom accounts. An editor, legend has that it was Tertullian, took her story "according to her own ideas and in the way that she herself wrote it down," and gave it the title "Passion of Perpetua and Felicitas."

We think of preaching in the early church the way Justin Martyr described it (c. 165): On Sunday, "The memoirs of the apostles or the writings of the prophets are read as long as time permits. When the reader has finished, the president in a discourse urges and invites [us] to the imitation of these noble things. Then we all stand up together and offer prayers."[1]

Perpetua's story does not fit this description. Nonetheless, there are good reasons for reclaiming Perpetua and the early martyrs as preachers:

1) Martyrdom was considered the highest form of Christian witness. In fact, the Greek of the New Testament uses the same word for witness and martyr. The rationale Justin Martyr is said to have given at his trial is typical of the doctrinal basis the early church adopted for this form of proclamation: "We are confident that if we suffer the penalty for the sake of our Lord Jesus Christ we shall be saved, for this is the confidence and salvation we shall have at the terrible tribunal of our Saviour and Master sitting in judgement over the whole world."[2]

2) The martyrs proclaimed their faith in the face of their accusers, in the prisons, in the courts, before the crowds in the amphitheaters, and, as in Perpetua's writing, before the whole world.

3) The cumulative historical impact of the martyrs' unique form of proclamation was pervasive for four centuries. The martyrs found in the life of Christ a model for sacrificing one's own life that was an effective alternative to armed uprising. They fueled the view that the function of the state was to be handmaiden to the church.

Sermon Sample

Two aspects of Perpetua's preaching form deserve particular sampling here. One is the *autobiographical* form:

What a difficult time it was! With the crowd the heat was stifling; then there was the extortion of the soldiers; and to crown it all, I was tortured with worry for my baby there. . . . Then I got permission for my baby to stay with me in prison. At once I recovered my health, relieved as I was of my worry and anxiety over the child. My prison had suddenly become a palace. . . .

Hilarianus the governor . . . said to me: "Have pity on your father's grey head; have pity on your infant son. Offer the sacrifice for the welfare of the emperors."

"I will not," I retorted.

"Are you a Christian?" said Hilarianus.

And I said: "Yes, I am."

When my father persisted in trying to dissuade me, Hilarianus ordered him to be thrown to the ground and beaten with a rod. I felt sorry for father, just as if I myself had been beaten.[3]

The other homiletical form of interest is *apocalyptic*, used in recounting her visions. Here is a portion of her famous first vision (on which Augustine preached—Sermon 280), from which she predicts that they will be condemned, that Saturus will be the first of their group to die, and that she will also be victorious in her upcoming battle with the devil:

At the foot of the ladder lay a dragon of enormous size, and it would attack those who tried to climb up and try to terrify them from doing so. And Saturus was the first to go up. . . . He had been the builder of our strength. . . . And he arrived at the top of the staircase and he looked back and said to me: "Perpetua, I am waiting for you. But take care; do not let the dragon bite you."

"He will not harm me," I said, "in the name of Christ Jesus."

Slowly, as though he were afraid of me, the dragon stuck his head out from underneath the ladder. Then, by using it as my first step, I trod on his head and went up.[4]

Implications

Perpetua's story retains such power over the centuries not only because of the horror of her circumstances but also because of the honest self-disclosure of her prose. She focuses on relationships. Her use of actual conversations and brief identification of her own feelings is important in re-creating the scenes for us. Richard Thulin has shown in his *The "I" of the Sermon* that autobiography continues to be a powerful medium for preaching.[5]

Many aspects of the martyrdom movement in the early church are troubling to us. Recall though that Perpetua's story of persecution is similar in function to Anne Frank's *Diary*. Perpetua's story was used by the early church to reflect on the suffering of Christ. There are many stories of persecution today that need to be heard from the pulpit, in some instances as testimonies of Christian faith, and in some instances as testimonies against evil.

Apocalyptic preaching of the regrettable sort may make a resurgence as this millennium draws to a close. Perpetua's visions of the end times need not be placed in the camp of those who would eagerly anticipate nuclear holocaust as the Second Coming. Rather, Perpetua's visions may be understood as visions of the realm of God that were helpful to her and her companions, in a culture profoundly different from our own, and in the midst of desperate circumstances. Perhaps we too could describe, in our preaching, dreams and visions of what God's realm might look like when it breaks in today or tomorrow, dreams that nurture our faith and hope. In other words, in our preaching we do not need merely to list incidents of brokenness and sin in the world. This sort of recital may be important not least in naming the powers of this world. But to leave it there is to say yes to those same powers, as if they have final say. Instead, frequently try picturing in the sermons the same scene, this time showing what it might look like if God's will were being done, and picture it in detail provided by imagination and faith.

THE EAST: A WORD GIVES VARIETIES OF MEANING

CHAPTER 3

Origen (185–254)
Alexandria and Allegory

Origen grew up in Alexandria, the large Mediterranean port city on the western reaches of the Nile delta in Egypt. This was the location of the famous Library; the place where seventy-two scholars had first translated the Jewish scriptures into Greek (hence Septuagint); the place where Mark is credited with starting a church; the place where Philo (d. c. 50) had taught a method of harmonizing Jewish thought and Greek philosophy; and where Clement (d. 215) used similar Christian approaches in teaching at the catechetical school attached to the cathedral. Origen had read widely in philosophy and literature before he came to study with Clement.

When Origen was eighteen an edict was enacted aimed at any of the proselytizing religions. Christians, until the fifth century, were in aggressive competition with Jews for pagan converts. Origen would have joined his father in martyrdom, but his mother hid his clothes and presumably anything else he might have draped over his body, preventing his leaving home on the fateful day. Clement, his teacher, was forced to flee, and Origen was appointed head of the school.

Asceticism was part of the philosophy of his day, but it alone does not explain why, once he found himself teaching, he found it necessary to castrate himself. His enemies in the church later used this action against him, and from Eusebius on, historians have joked that the great teacher of allegory could only read Matthew 19:12 ("eunuchs for the sake of the kingdom") literally. He was a lay-preacher in Caesarea prior to being ordained there. As his academic reputation grew, he traveled widely, preaching and teaching in Caesarea, Jerusalem, and elsewhere.

When Emperor Decius came to power (249–251) there was a massive persecution of Christians and Jews. Origen survived torture but died four years later. We know him for his Bible commentaries, his homilies, and as the first systematic theologian of the church.

Homiletical Setting

Jerome lists for Origen 444 Old Testament sermons and 130 for the New, but only a third of the total survive. Of these, only 21 (primarily his series on Jeremiah) survive in the Greek and are an accurate reflection of both his content and style. The rest underwent some abridgment at the time of translation into Latin. Some dispute Eusebius' claim that it was only when Origen was sixty that he allowed his sermons to be written down in shorthand and published.[1]

Several ideas give shape to Alexandrian homiletics, many of which may be found in Book Four of Origen's *On First Principles.*

1) The success of the Christian movement is a proof of its truth. The Old Testament is revelation only insofar as it is prophetic of Christ. Jesus "reads it to us." The exegete is to find the harmony between the Hebrew Scriptures and the evangelists and apostles. The image of Christ, the church, the new covenant, and the like are prefigured as *types* or models. Thus for Origen, Joshua becomes a *type*

of his namesake, Jesus Christ, and Joshua's life is a commentary on our life.

2) Revelation is hidden in the Scriptures. The masses of common people cannot expect to understand. We progress from knowledge of the small and visible to knowledge of the great and invisible, from the bodily and sensual to the spiritual and intellectual.

3) As with Philo and earlier Jewish scholars, the word is the unit of meaning. It both discloses meaning to the discerner and hides meaning from those unable to read it correctly. Since God would not have wasted dictation of a single dot, or syllable, or word, each has an intent and purpose.

4) Scripture is written symbolically. It is more like poetry than prose. It is like a coded message from God that can be unlocked with the best tools of science and art used by the Stoics, Philo, and others. These included Greek philosophy, arithmetic (numbers have divine meanings); etymology (the true meaning may be hidden in the root of a word); riddles or parables (applied correctly, the actual meaning of the passage is revealed); and most of all typology and *allegory* (details in a biblical text had one-to-one correspondence with truths revealed by Christ). Allegorical interpretations were put there by God for Christians to discern.

5) The individual word for Origen is "free-floating," loosed from history and what we would consider to be the moors of adjacent sentences and paragraphs. Instead, allegory functions as the word's context. Origen uses allegory in part to rescue difficult passages in the scriptures from charges of being amoral, trivial, or absurd.

6) The scriptures have three senses: the Word has a "flesh" or literal sense that helps the common people to avoid error; the Word has a "soul" or moral sense that awakens the human soul to holy life; and the Word has a "spirit" or mystical-eschatological sense that brings a per-

son to union with God and truth (*Principles*, 4:11). In practice Origen rarely distinguishes between the latter two. Nor does he give primary importance to the literal sense: Often for him it is simply a rudimentary interpretation in need of further understanding.

7) When the literal ("flesh," "obvious," "corporeal," or "material") sense runs into problems or stumbling blocks, it is a signal of a spiritual meaning to be discovered (4:15). Not all Scripture has a literal sense, for it includes irrational events that do not make sense: the Garden of Eden; Noah's Ark; Jesus being tempted from such a great height as to be able to see India; the heavenly Jerusalem.

8) The key to correct interpretation lies in the spirituality and knowledge of the interpreter. The wild excesses and exaggerated subtlety of his approach, seen in his commentaries, were one way of avoiding some of the dangers of a strictly literal reading.

Origen's typology seems simply arbitrary to us, and his "science" seems akin to astrology, as it did to some of his contemporaries. His immediate legacy was to make Christian thought acceptable and even attractive to the Greek mind. Unfortunately, with his commentaries and other writings, he helped to secure the church's move in the direction of allegory and typology for the next thousand years and beyond. But he also gave us a less frequently noted gift in being critical of the literal.

Sermon Sample

Origen typically represents God as the loving teacher. This homily is based on Jeremiah 18:7-10, in which God says that if a condemned nation repents, "I will repent of the evil that I intended to do to it." His overall argument unfurls beautifully: God speaks of repenting; God is not like humans; God merely adopts our way of speaking.

But God, who foreknows the future, cannot have made bad decisions and repent on that score. . . . But when . . . God is involved with the affairs of men, then he takes on the mind, the ways and the speech of a man. When we talk to a two-year-old, we use baby language for the child's sake. . . . You will find many more similar examples of God bearing the ways of man. If you hear of God's anger and his wrath, do not think of wrath and anger as emotions experienced by God. Accommodations of the use of language like that are designed for the correction and improvement of the little child. We too put on a severe face for children not because that is our true feeling but because we are accommodating ourselves to their level. . . . So God is said to be wrathful and declares that he is angry in order that you may be corrected and improved. But God is not really wrathful or angry. Yet you will experience the effects of wrath and anger, through finding yourself in trouble that can scarcely be borne on account of your wickedness, when you are being disciplined by the so-called wrath of God.[2]

Implications

Origen rejects the literal idea of God repenting, which is inconsistent with his doctrine of the perfection of God. It is a simple example of a common practice in the church: Doctrine often takes precedence in the act of interpretation.

His extended simile of "the kind parent with the child" promotes the idea of a tender loving God. Our own idea of God is affected by Origen's image as we listen, but so is our idea of Origen. Instead of someone who may seem intellectually remote and distant, he seems approachable and loving. How we speak of God in our preaching is very important, because it affects our pastoral relationships. We might try listing the various images we have of God in our own devotional life. How would you characterize the images you list? Are they warm or cold? loving or stern? nurturing or reproving? We might then go back over our sermons to see what kind of images and language we have actually used to speak of God. Is there a discrepancy between our personal and our public vocabulary? Is there a difference between the words that we use when we speak from the heart and those when we speak from the head?

Elsewhere in his sermon, Origen asked God two questions. This is an excellent device used to effective purpose. His questions represent our questions, our doubts, and by asking them he encourages us to take our own concerns directly to God. Many people think that their questions, doubts, disappointments, anger do not belong with God. Of course this is not the case, as the psalmist teaches us. By briefly moving his focus in this manner from us to God, Origen communicates a sense of God's immediacy and presence. It is as though God might actually be listening and might be part of our gathering together. It is almost as though God cares, which is, in fact, the truth.

CHAPTER 4

Chrysostom (c. 347–407)
Antioch and the Literal

Antioch, unlike Alexandria, had a formal theological school. An architecturally stunning Syrian city on the trade route, it lay on a narrow strip of fertile land between the Orontes River and a chain of mountains, twenty miles from the Mediterranean. Here followers of Christ were first called Christians (Acts 11:26). Many Christians here worshiped in the synagogues, celebrated Jewish festivals, and generally regarded the Jewish faith as more potent spiritually than their own. Christianity was now the favored state religion (323) and had monetary wealth as well as estates from which it ministered to the needs of 3,000 persons. Many sought church vocations for the wrong reasons. Devout Christians throughout the East held in high spiritual regard the religious hermits in Antioch's surrounding mountains.

John Chrysostom (= of the golden mouth) was given his name long after his death. Born to noble and wealthy parents, he was reared in the church by his mother, Anthusa. After her death in 375, he began six years of studying Scripture by living as a hermit, four of them under the direction of an old monk, and two of them alone in a cave. When his health suffered, he returned to Antioch where he was ordained first as a deacon in 381 and then as a presbyter in 386. His vivid series of twenty-one sermons, "On the Statues," during a tax revolt of 387, earned him large followings, and he became the great preacher of Antioch for the next twelve years.

The royal court forced him to accept the position of bishop and patriarch of the relatively new capital city, Constantinople. Enemies, headed by the patriarch of Alexandria and largely jealous of Constantinople's rightful claim to be the "New Rome" of the East, removed him *in absentia* from office at an illegal synod in 403. The empress, whom he had already offended in preaching about Jezebel, was sufficiently superstitious about the timing of an earthquake that she went with the crowd's wish and reinstated him. When he criticized a silver statue of her erected next to his cathedral, her superstition was overcome and she banished him to an isolated village on the eastern Black Sea. He corresponded frequently, leaving more than 200 letters, and died in exile.

Homiletical Setting

Chrysostom's *Treatise on the Priesthood* gave this homiletical guidance: The primary task is to deliver God's Word and to look for God's approval, remaining indifferent to applause and praise. Priests were not to steal material from other preachers or to be suspected of this kind of thievery. Ironically, the Trullo Council, three centuries later in 692, reversed this and directed preachers not to compose their own homilies but to model themselves on Chrysostom and two Cappadocian contemporaries, Gregory of Nazianzus and Basil.[1] Sermon anthologies of all three received wide use through the Middle Ages, and some Orthodox churches still use one of Chrysostom's homilies on Easter Sunday.

His surviving sermons number in excess of 600. Most are from his time in Antioch where they were transcribed by private stenographers. From their length it is assumed that he normally preached for at least an hour. Some of his sermons are the most readable of the ones that come to us from the early church. Some, particularly those attacking the Jews, are among the most intolerable.

Antioch and Alexandria differed greatly:

1) Chrysostom found no truth in non-Christian sources. Consequently the Old Testament is now claimed as the rightful possession of Christians, not Jews. The Scriptures impart no holiness "to the defiled" (Homily 1:6).

2) He prefers reason to philosophy in the act of interpretation. His approach is literal, favoring the grammatical (i.e., common sense) and historical (i.e., traditionally accepted) meaning of Scripture. The obvious meaning of a metaphor is part of the literal meaning of a text; thus, the presence of a metaphor is not a signal of allegorical intent. He uses allegory only when the biblical writer says it is intended.

3) The Old Testament is prophetic of Christ, not about Christ, and Christ is not read back into it. It is taken as a form of history, not as symbols. Chrysostom is less concerned with the biblical writers in their own times than with what they are saying to his time. Thus Jewish feast days are no longer to be observed, "For since the Truth is come, the Types have no longer any place" (Homily 14:8).

4) Antioch followed Jewish principles of interpreting the law for today, including those mentioned earlier: moving from the simple to the difficult, from the lesser to the greater, from like to like, from general to particular or particular to general, using one passage with another, and consideration of the surrounding context.[2]

Chrysostom's homiletic is pastoral and popular. It is blended with social justice themes about wealth and the ideals of charity that are inspired by his asceticism. His constant bias is for the poor. His preaching assumes the authority of the church, even as he says it is a sin to question the priest: "But dost thou suspect the priest?" he asks, preaching on wealth, "Why this thing in itself, to begin with, is a grievous sin." He laments that there are corrupt priests, but "even if thou hast a bad teacher, this will not avail thee, shouldest thou not attend to the things that are spoken" (Homily 21:11).

The form and structure of his homilies ranges from nonbiblical narrative about contemporary life to a form of exegetical preaching in which he may casually move from verse to verse or from one text to another. His background is rhetoric, but he is unconcerned with tight arguments or with sticking to a precise theme or text, matters normally having to do with the classical rhetorical canon of Arrangement.

Sermon Sample

When in February of 387 the people of Antioch rioted against new taxes and desecrated the statues of the emperor, punishment came in the form of tribunals, imprisonment, torture, and death of many of the city's leaders. It was fully possible that the emperor would order the entire splendid city to be destroyed. Just prior to the trial Chrysostom preaches:

At the present time then, a man [the emperor] is angry with us, a man of like passions, and of like soul, and we are afraid: but in the case of Job it was an evil and malignant demon who was angry . . . and brought forward every stratagem; and yet even with all he could not conquer the fortitude of the just man. But here is a man, who is at one time angry, at another time is reconciled; and we are nevertheless dead with fear. . . . What apology then, or what pardon can be ours, if we cannot sustain a human trial; we who are taught such spiritual wisdom under grace; when this man [Job] before grace, and before the Old Testament, endured this most grievous war so nobly! These things, beloved, we should therefore always discourse of with one another; and by words of this kind encourage ourselves.[3]

Another sermon gives an excellent sampling of his use of doctrine and rhetoric:

Adam committed one sin, and brought on total death. We commit a thousand sins every day. If by committing a single sin he brought such terrible evil on himself and introduced death into the world, what should we, who live continually in sin, expect to suffer . . .? This is a burdensome message; it does upset the man who hears it. I know, because I feel it myself. I am disturbed by it; it makes me quake. The clearer the proofs I find of this message of hell, the more I tremble and melt with fear. But I have to proclaim it so that we may not fall into hell. . . . I ask you to bear with these words of fire. Perhaps, yes, perhaps, they may bring you some consolation. . . . If God had given you commandments that were burdensome or impossible to fulfil, someone might possibly have pleaded the difficulty of the laws. But if they are easy of fulfillment, what excuse can we offer when even so we fail to keep them? You cannot fast or practise celibacy, you say. But you could if you so wished, and those who have succeeded in doing so are our accusers. . . . Then you will argue that you cannot give away all of your possessions. But you could—and those who do so are proof of it. Yet here again this is not something that God has laid on us. His command is that you should not be grasping and that you should provide for the needy out of what you have. And if anyone says, "I cannot be content with my wife alone," he is self-deceiving and his claim is false. . . . It is doing these things that is burdensome, not refraining from them.[4]

Implications

When his city was facing the possibility of destruction on an apocalyptic scale, Chrysostom continued to preach a message of hope. It was not the foolish hope that everything will go away, but a hope for courage, strength, and mutual support that still keeps open the possibility of God's intervention. Our own world seems to face a variety of apocalyptic scenarios, and our media seems to find new ones each day. Numerous death scenarios spread before us: nuclear, greenhouse, defoliation, pollution, disease. They are real and they are serious. We must learn to change the way we live, not seeking greater wealth through progress but seeking greater love through justice. In our preaching we can ignore the big issues, but our people will still bring them to the service in one way or another. How much better it is to acknowledge what they are struggling with, as Chrysostom did with his people. We do as he did: Because of our faith we never give in to the "worst case scenario" and always preach hope. Much of the power of Chrysostom's message comes from a willingness to bring politics and world events before God's Word.

We might also learn, in the second selection just given, from the way he identifies his own personal difficulty with the truth he is proclaiming. Given his tough message, this makes it easier to stay listening to him. He anticipates our questions and encourages our anxiety about his topic as he continues to develop his doctrine of divine punishment. Only when he senses that we have no more defense does he begin to build some hope in the form of practical things we may do. This is good theological communication. We might allow the burden of God's word to unfold fully before we begin to expound God's grace. Overall unity is strengthened by use of the word "burdensome," which occurs three times in the passage.

CHAPTER 5

Romanos the Melodist (c. 490–c. 560)
Constantinople and Poetry

Little is known of this amazing preacher's life,
although Romanos is the greatest of the poet-preachers in
the Eastern church and one of the great religious poets of
all time. Born near Beirut of Jewish parents, he was in
Constantinople to witness the riot in 532 that destroyed
the old St. Sophia Cathedral (where Chrysostom had
preached) and the eventual rebuilding of the present
magnificent cathedral. He created a form of metrical sermon that by the ninth century was called the Kontakion.
The name came from the particular kind of staff around
which the surviving scrolls of his sermons were preserved.

The Council of Chalcedon in 451 made final the doctrine but not the controversy about the nature of Christ,
particularly in the East. During the last half of Romanos'
life, the emperors began to insist upon and enforce the
Chalcedon position. Romanos' metrical sermons met two
needs: an attraction away from the theater and circus,
particularly on feast days, and reinforcement of the
emperor's theology.

An ancient biographer for the church calendar says that
Romanos received the gift of composing the kontakion
from the Virgin Mary, who appeared to him in a dream
during a Christmas Eve all-night vigil. She gave him a
piece of paper he was to eat. On consuming it he awoke,

mounted the pulpit, and sang a sermon, "On the Nativity I" (on Mary and the Magi). His kontakia found their way into the regular liturgy of the Eastern church, in which he became a saint. Eventually they were presented with elaborate artistic backdrops and were removed from the liturgy in the iconoclastic movement of the eighth century. They continued to be performed in other locations such as the Imperial Palace in Constantinople, at least until the twelfth century.[1] By the close of the first millennium, his sermons had influenced the creation of sacred "mysteries" and the rebirth of theater in the West.

Homiletical Setting

Romanos may have written more than 1,000 kontakia, but only 59 genuine ones survive. They were preached at the morning office of the day, not at the mass. Sometimes they followed the reading of the Gospel directly, but at other times they were preceded by a prose homily.

Discovery of the "Homily on the Passion" by Bishop Melito of Sardis, who lived in West Asia Minor around 165, has led scholars to believe that there was an unbroken tradition of sermons with meter and rhyme, perhaps originating with the Psalms. Augustine's sermons, if read in the original Latin, frequently have rhyme, parallelism, antithesis, assonance, and wordplay. St. Paulinus of Nola (353–431), a bishop in France, wrote extensive poetry that may have had homiletical use. Nothing in the West, however, compares with the poem-sermons of Ephrem (c. 306–c. 373), Romanos, and, later, John of Damascus (c. 675–c. 749). Each devised his own personal, distinctive form set to music that is now lost.

A contemporary of Romanos wrote under the pseudonym of Dionysius the Areopagite between 500 and 510. His Heavenly Hierarchy draws heavily upon

Plato's *Timaeus* and set the standard for liturgical art in the East.[2] He says that the music of the church is transmitted to humans from the heavenly choirs. The singing of the church brings the congregation into harmony with the liturgy, with God, with oneself, and with one's neighbor. Artists are merely humble instruments of God, which may be why Romanos calls himself "the humble" and why we know almost nothing about his life from his sermons. Moreover, artists are not to compose freely but are to pattern themselves on the heavenly images that have already been transmitted to the church. Thus icons were to capture the previous inherited "idea" of the saints, not the actual resemblance. Similarly Eastern sermons, after the Trullo Council of 692, were to imitate those of the earlier great preachers.

Romanos' poem-sermons have an introduction followed usually by twenty-four stanzas of identical design, even to the number of syllables in each line. The preacher-narrator takes us from beginning to end through the biblical story being preached. Along the way he is also the voice for two or three other characters or groups. Each character or group is given a sustained focus and opportunity to speak. The drama and the theology is of the utmost simplicity and clarity. Information and moral instruction are placed in the mouth of one of the speakers. By the end of the sermon, the congregation has heard the choir sing the same refrain, which functions as the sermon's central idea, at least twenty-five times and would be joining in. Some of these intriguing refrains include: "Savior, save me"; "The Master of all"; "Hasten, Holy One, save Thy sheep"; "Crying, 'Open'"; and "He who is everywhere and fills all things."

Romanos brings a new emotive dimension to sermons through his poetry and music. Individual words and sounds are not free-floating but are tied into the larger harmony and unity of the whole. This unity in music also represents the church. In his sermon on Elijah, he comes dangerously close to claiming that God is bound by the words of the prophet-preacher. He represents an important step toward the mystical preaching of the Middle Ages, for instance toward the Eastern hymns and sermons of St. Symeon The New Theologian (949–1022). At the same time he is an important forerunner of African American preaching and narrative preaching today.

Sermon Sample

Romanos' most famous sermon and his only Epiphany kontakion, "On the Presentation in the Temple," is not his most poetic, but it is an excellent example of his use of doctrine, emphasizing the two natures of Christ. The refrain is "Thou, the only friend of man." In addition to the preacher, the characters are Mary, Simeon, and Christ. Here are stanzas three and four, which are best read aloud:

While the angels sang hymns to the lover of men, Mary advanced,
Holding Him in her arms;
And she pondered on how she became mother and remained a virgin,
For she realized that the birth was supernatural; she was awed and she trembled.
Meditating on these things, she said to herself:
"How shall I find a name for Thee, my son?
For if I call Thee the man I see Thou art, yet Thou art more than man.
Thou hast kept my virginity unsullied,
Thou, the only friend of man.

. . . .

"Shall I call Thee perfect man? But I know that Thy conception was divine,
For no mortal man
Was ever conceived without intercourse and seed as Thou,
O blameless One.
And if I call Thee God, I am amazed at seeing Thee in every respect like me,
For Thou hast no traits which differ from those of man,
Yet Thou wast conceived and born without sin.
Shall I give Thee milk, or worship Thee, for Thy deeds
Proclaim Thee God beyond time, even after Thou didst become man?
Thou, the only friend of man."[3]

Christ later responds to Simeon's prayer to depart in peace by promising him release from the temporal world. Then Christ addresses the congregation, "Soon I shall appear, redeeming all of you/I the only friend of man." In the final stanza, Romanos prays a prayer of protection for all of us.

Implications

We can be attentive to a number of features in Romanos' preaching.

1) Partly because of the discipline imposed on him by his music, he takes great care in selecting each word. Every word is important. The result is an economy and beauty of expression that has power.
2) There is no mistaking his simple central idea, to which he keeps returning. Our central ideas would benefit from being as clear and as memorable, although if we are wishing to focus on the actions of God, as we should, we would be wise to make God the subject of our sentence (the central idea).

3) Romanos keeps the number of characters to a minimum. Like any good storyteller, he locates them in one place, and additional important information is given in retrospective or anticipatory thinking.

4) He makes excellent use of dialogue to compress his thought and to avoid much theological qualification.

5) He allows the characters to speak and thereby lets us "overhear" instead of telling us what we "must hear."

6) The device of putting words directly in the mouth of Christ has a strong, loving, pastoral effect. We hear this as Christ speaking personally to us.

Although Romanos is dealing with controversial theological issues of his day, his overall effect is to assure his listeners that living a faithful life, in the midst of the controversy, is sufficient. The same is true of all ages.

THE WEST:
THE CONTROLLED WORD

CHAPTER 6

Cyprian (200–258)
Carthage and Authoritative Exegesis

Cyprian was a wealthy legal advocate and a professional teacher of rhetoric. He was forty-five when he was baptized, was ordained shortly thereafter, and, with a swiftness that makes modern heads turn as it did ancient, was elected and consecrated Bishop of Carthage, with significant opposition, in 249 while still a novice. Decius became emperor in the same year, and the edict under which Origen was tortured took effect on January 1, 250. In response, Cyprian had a vision that told him to go into hiding for a year in order to care for his people, which he did largely through epistles. It was only six years before another edict was issued under which Cyprian was exiled for a year and then beheaded as a martyr on September 14, 258.

He was a fiery man of remarkable generosity and compassion. Early in his faith he sold his estates and distributed his wealth to care for the poor. When the city of Carthage was ravaged by a plague and people in fear were casting even their own ill friends out into the streets to fend for themselves, Cyprian spearheaded a mission to care for anyone in need.

Several important church controversies arose in quick succession during his time, and on each he took a firm stand. Initially he seemed hesitant to claim much ecclesial power, but after Novatian wrongly claimed to be bishop of Rome, he forcefully asserted the apostolic authority of the rightful bishops in his text *The Unity of the Catholic Church*. The Novatian sect was heretical, outside the church. In his words: "The spouse of Christ cannot be adulterous; she is uncorrupted and pure. She knows one home; she guards with chaste modesty the sanctity of one couch. She keeps us for God. Whoever is separated from the Church and is joined to an adulteress . . . is an enemy. He can no longer have God for his Father, who has not the Church for his mother" (sec. 6). Sacraments given outside the Spirit-filled church were no sacraments.

The Latin church in the West was slower to develop than the Greek church for various reasons including language and geography. Cyprian, and before him Tertullian, was an early, important, and lasting voice in establishing the authority of the church.

Homiletical Setting

Cyprian wrote 65 epistles and 12 treatises, the latter generally being recognized as sermons, exhortations, and collections of scriptural "proof texts." As is often the case in the early church, the lines between these are not clear.

In adapting rhetoric to the pulpit, Cyprian said that preachers, unlike lawyers in court, should aim at "a chaste simplicity" that uses truth, not eloquence, for conviction: "not clever but weighty words, not decked up to charm a popular audience with cultivated rhetoric, but simple and fitted by their unvarnished truthfulness for the proclamation of divine mercy" (Letter to Donatus: 2).

Ignatius of Antioch (c. 110) had maintained that the local bishop is the focus of unity and is God's representative on earth. Tertullian (d. c. 220) had refused to heretics any right to interpret Scripture—before he became one himself! Cyprian goes one step farther: The authority was in the church, ensured by the bishops in their line of apostolic succession. The authority of the bishops "forms a unity" which they transmit to the church.

With Cyprian's work there arose the assumption of an *authoritative interpretation* of Scripture.[1] It was essential for deciding on what grounds a doctrine could be refuted. Anyone could quote Scripture to find support, but who was right? Authoritative interpretation comes from the received oral tradition. It rests as much outside Scripture as within it, for as long as allegory is to reign and words are not tightly fastened to their context, internal textual evidence of "correct" and "incorrect" interpretation cannot be found. The church had to decide using the simple rule of faith: Scripture means what the church says it means. Cyprian uses allegory when the literal sense does not make sense and is not defined by tradition.

Every time he quotes Scripture in his writings, he indicates that he is quoting. Scripture speaks directly, in the present tense, predicting the precise situations that are happening in his current-day Carthage.[2] Other features of his homiletic seem simply idiosyncratic to his time: Individual words, numbers, and insignificant details spark doctrinal discussion; a play on words in his Latin Bible is worth expounding; and one small idea can lead to many diverse scriptural texts.

Cyprian is a strong perpetuator of the anti-Semitism that stains Christian history and much preaching to the present day. His *Three Books of Testimonies Against the Jews* (in the tradition of Justin Martyr's *Dialogue with Tryphon*) takes many of the central tenets of the Christian faith and finds them all foretold many times in the ancient Scriptures.

Sermon Sample

Cyprian's treatise *On the Lord's Prayer*, modeled on Tertullian's book on prayer, is often quoted by Augustine. It is either one sermon in three parts or a series of three sermons. The first part is on Christ's general admonition to pray. The second is a superb example of early exegetical preaching, taking the Lord's Prayer clause by clause and expounding its message. The third part is instruction on how we are to pray as a church.

The first sentence of each paragraph identifies the theme of the paragraph, and the paragraph does not stray beyond its theme. Thus the first section, for example, progresses smoothly as follows: (1) The teachings of the evangelists are divine teachings; (2) Christ instructed us for what to pray; (3) let us pray as God has taught us; (4) let our prayer be quiet and modest under the church's discipline; (5) Hannah was a type of the church; (6) remember the Pharisee praying in the temple; (7) we are to pray the Lord's Prayer.

The following is an extract:

Hannah in the first book of Kings was a type of the Church . . . in that she prayed to God not with clamorous petition, but silently and modestly, within the very recesses of her heart. She spoke with hidden prayer, but with manifest faith. She spoke not with her voice, but with her heart, because she knew that thus God hears; and she effectually obtained what she sought, because she asked it with belief. Divine Scripture asserts this, when it says, "She spake in her heart, and her lips moved, and her voice was not heard." [I Sam. 1:13; he goes on to quote two other passages from Psalm 4:4 and Baruch 4:6][3]

In this next section he deals with the first clause of the prayer:

For we say not "My Father, which art in heaven," nor "Give me this day my daily bread;" nor does each one ask only his own debt should be forgiven him; nor does he request for himself alone that he may not be led into temptation, and delivered from evil. Our prayer is public and common; and when we pray, we pray not for one, but for the whole people, because we the whole people are one. The God of peace and the Teacher of concord, who taught unity, willed that one should thus pray for all, even as He Himself bore us all in one. This law of prayer the three children observed when they were shut up in the fiery furnace, speaking together in prayer, and being of one heart in the agreement of the spirit. . . . [he quotes the scripture passage] Thus also we find that the apostles, with the disciples, prayed after the Lord's ascension: "They all," says the Scripture, "continued with one accord in prayer, with the women, and Mary who was the mother of Jesus, and with His brethren."[4]

Implications

The problem with allegorical typology for us is theological. It reads Christ back into the Old Testament and makes the text bend to whatever Christian meaning we might seek to take to it. We force an identity upon the text that is not its own. But we can learn something from ancient typology. Our age is appropriately more comfortable with metaphor and simile. How different Cyprian sounds to our ears if instead of saying Hannah "is a type of the church" he says, Hannah "can be understood to be like the church." The meaning is not forced and the Hannah text can retain its own identity if handled properly.

Cyprian was famous for the clarity of his thinking. He is easy on our ears because his thoughts are ordered and seem simple. One thought consistently leads on to the next. This is not the three-point sermon thinking that some unfortunately have come to identify with rhetoric. Rather it is discourse that cares about the listener, moving step by step. We might wish to experiment with the exegetical form, perhaps even imitating for our own time what Cyprian did with the Lord's Prayer. In addition, however, we could follow Cyprian's method for clarity: The opening sentence of each paragraph identifies the paragraph's subject, each paragraph does not go beyond that boundary, and each paragraph flows into the next.

The idea of an authoritative interpretation of Scripture is not something that warms the modern heart, not only because it has proved to be illusive, but also because, when some have claimed to have it, it has often been used in an authoritarian manner. Preachers learn that there are many correct interpretations of any one text. The authoritative interpretation today is not singular or universal. It is informed by scholarship. It is affirmed by the community of the church. It is confirmed in the lives of the faithful today. And it is sensitive to the needs of others. In our preaching we should never claim for our own interpretation more or less authority than this. Rather than claim authority, our task is to lead our people to a recognition of the One authority who claims each of us.

CHAPTER 7

Augustine (354–430)
Hippo and the Primacy of the Rule of Love

By Augustine's time the great persecutions had ended (the last was in 304). Born near Carthage to a family of modest means, he was reared by his mother in the church. His autobiography, *Confessions,* tells of wild student living; teaching rhetoric for nine years during which he followed Manichaeism, a sect that explained the universe as a conflict of light and dark; having a son in 372 by the woman with whom he was living; moving with them to Rome and Milan in 383–384 to teach rhetoric; listening to Ambrose preach and becoming a catechumen; sending his partner back home at the urging of his mother; taking another woman as partner; forswearing marriage and going into retreat for a year; and finally, with his son, being baptized by Ambrose at Easter in 387. Shortly thereafter he returned to North Africa, gave his possessions to the poor, began a monastic life, and experienced his son's early tragic death.

The rest of Augustine's life may seem somewhat dull by comparison. Ordained in spite of his "protests and weeping" while visiting Hippo in 391, he began to preach at his bishop's request and to study the Scriptures. He addressed the Council of Hippo in 393, which confirmed the scriptural canon. At age forty-one he became bishop of Hippo, traveled widely, wrote extensively, and was soon at the forefront of the intellectual life of the church. He died at age seventy-six.

Prior to meeting Ambrose, Augustine had no patience for the Scriptures or for their attributing human form to God. Ambrose was an orator, a man of learning, and a former governor, elected bishop by the people of Milan while yet unbaptized. He introduced Augustine to Neoplatonic ideals of mystical union with truth, and to the allegorical interpretations of Origen and others. Augustine found he could accept that humans are made in the spiritual image of God. He began searching out the "invisible things" of God. Ambrose pointed Augustine to evidence of the Trinity in the Greek philosophers. Through philosophy Ambrose gave him something he desperately wanted—a way of reading the Old Testament that he could find intellectually respectable.

Augustine's writings include critiques of his former sect; attacks on Donatists who maintained (with Cyprian) that the validity of the sacraments was dependent upon the orthodoxy of the priest; and polemics against Pelagius, a monk from Britain who affirmed free will and denied original sin and the need for prevenient grace. Augustine's *On Christian Doctrine* is the first and the most influential homiletical textbook in Christian history.

Homiletical Setting

As a written document, *On Christian Doctrine* set firm standards that became, with other written documents and creeds, the new orthodoxy that was increasingly linked with the page. Augustine uses the word *doctrine* in his title to refer to both the content and form of preaching. His first three chapters speak about sound biblical interpretation, and the fourth is primarily classical rhetoric adapted for the Christian preacher. Of 1,535 sermons attributed to him, 683 survive along with 100 treatises and 200 letters. Many of the sermons were originally transcribed by stenographers or *notarii* who sat at the front of the sanctuary.

The sermons vary greatly in form. Many are exegetical (e.g., his commentary on the Psalms). Many are doctrinal with no specific biblical text. We may highlight several aspects of his homiletic that become a new orthodoxy for the church:

1) Typical exegesis is found in his sermon "The Recovering of Sight to the Blind" (Matt. 20:30). Augustine notes that Jesus was passing by, yet he stood still to heal: "What is *Jesus passeth by?* Jesus is doing things which last but for a time. What is *Jesus passeth by?* Jesus doth things which pass by. Mark and see how many things of His have *passed by.* He was born of the Virgin Mary; is He being born always?"

2) He accepts four standard early church understandings of scripture, most of which form his underlying assumptions (cf. Irenaeus, d. 202, *Proof of the Apostolic Preaching*): The Old Testament is revealed in the New; the New Testament is disguised in the Old; the Old Testament is about Christ. The Gospels by now occupy a preeminent place in Scripture. Christ is "not a speaker who utters sounds exteriorly whom we consult" but is "the truth that presides within" the Scriptures (*On the Teacher,* 11:38).

3) The preacher sometimes heals by the application of similar things: "Because man fell through pride, He applied humility as a cure. . . . We ill used our immortality, so that we deserved to die; Christ used His mortality well to restore us." The principle of contraries is also used: "He was willing to give His life for ours when he had power to take it up again" (*On Christian Doctrine,* I:14, 15).[1]

4) Some subject matters in Scripture are meant to be taken literally ("openly"): "all those teachings which involve faith, the mores of living, and . . . hope and charity." These teachings illuminate "obscure" ("figurative," "allegorical," or "prophetic") texts (II:9). When a figurative text is understood literally it is being understood "carnally" and cannot edify the soul (III:5; 7). In interpreting a figurative text, check other translations and if necessary the original language (he knew no Hebrew). Translations that opt for ambiguity (i.e., aiming at a figurative, nonliteral reading) when clarity is possible are wrong (II:11; 12). The "rule of faith" (i.e., what the church has said) is to be applied in discerning ambiguous texts. If that still fails (and almost as a last resort!), consult the original "context" of the passage (III:2; 3).

5) The "knot . . . of . . . figurative action" may be "untied" using numbers or with a knowledge of music (II:14). This is to be distinguished from superstition or astrology (II:21), for the authority to interpret ambiguous "signs" correctly comes from the community: "Signs are not valid among men except by common consent" (II:24). When in doubt it is the authority of the "greater number" of catholic churches that is preferred (II:8). All truth is God's, although we may not gain access to it all. And though there are useful things to be learned from other literature, "If it is useful it is found here," in the Holy Scriptures (II:52).

6) The primary principle for interpretation of a figurative passage is *the rule of love* ("charity"); study the text "until an interpretation contributing to the reign of charity is produced" (III:15). Love is defined as "the motion of the soul toward the enjoyment of God for His sake, and the enjoyment of one's self and of one's neighbor for the sake of God" (III:10). Without this love, one cannot understand the Scriptures (I:36). It is in contrast to the rule of "cupidity" or self-love to which anything "concerning the bitterness or anger . . . of God" is addressed (III:11).

7) There are five spiritual steps that need to be taken by each person who would interpret Scripture correctly: fear of God, piety, knowledge, fortitude, and mercy (II:7). The latter is a reflection of *the primacy of God's grace* in overcoming our sin. God does not command without giving us the means with which to meet that command. Most of his sermons emphasize grace over law.

8) The purpose of the preaching is to teach, to delight, and to persuade (Cicero and Quintilian). Teaching is primary and the other two may naturally follow (IV:12ff.). The preacher "should not consider the eloquence of his teaching but the clarity of it" (IV:9). Sermons should not be prepared word for word and memorized, for that can mar effective communication (IV:10).

9) There are three ancient rhetorical styles of speaking: subdued, temperate, and grand (IV:17). Any one style may dominate any sermon, and the others are to be used to provide variety and prevent boredom. The grand style in preaching is not characterized by excessive ornament in language (as was the courtroom custom of the day), nor by applause, but by moving people to tears or to change their lives through an encounter with the truth (IV:22-24). (Cicero said in *Orator* [sec. 69] that the subdued or plain style was for proof [i.e., to teach], the temperate or middle style was for pleasure [i.e., to delight], and the grand was for emotion [i.e., to persuade or move].)

Augustine's *Confessions* is theology written in autobiographical style. It is curious that he excludes reference to personal or other experience from his actual preaching.

With Augustine the words of Scripture were not at the lawless control of those who chose to use them as they would. He and others like Pope Gregory the Great (*Pastoral Rule*, 591) became the standard authorities to consult in preparing to preach. Their approaches helped the church begin to control preaching and determine its development, instead of leaving it to the whim or ability of individual bishops.

Sermon Sample

In 275, the Emperor had instituted worship of the sun-god in a futile attempt to unite the empire. December 25, the Roman winter solstice, was set aside as a holiday to mark the birthdate of the sun-god. Christians in the West increasingly found it convenient to mark the day, adapting it to their own theology. Augustine preached both Christmas and Epiphany sermons, although he considers the principal feasts to be Passion, Resurrection, Ascension, and Pentecost. The following is from a Christmas sermon and probably would have been spoken in the "grand" style. This section, taken from his opening paragraph, is a prime example of his use of "contraries" and of poetic parallelism:

My mouth will speak the praise of the Lord. . . . He is great as the Day [i.e., God] of the angels, small in the day of men; the Word God before all time, the Word made flesh at a suitable time. Maker of the sun, he is made under the sun. Disposer of all ages in the bosom of the Father, He consecrates this day in the womb of His mother; in Him He remains, from her He goes forth. Creator of heaven and earth, He was born on earth under heaven. Unspeakably wise, He is wisely speechless; filling the world, He lies in a manger; Ruler of the stars, He nurses at His mother's bosom. He is both great in the nature of God and small in the form of a servant, but so that His greatness is not diminished by His smallness, nor His smallness overwhelmed by His greatness. For He did not desert His divine works when He took to Himself human members. Nor did He cease *to reach from end to end mightily, and to order all things sweetly* [cf. *Wisdom,* 8:1], when, having put on the infirmity of the flesh, He was received into the Virgin's womb, not confined therein.

After a passage of similar length in what might have been delivered in the subdued or temperate style, he returns to the grand style at the end of section 2:

... the Word of God, through which all things have been made ... which is not hemmed in by space, nor extended by time, nor varied by long and short pauses, nor composed by sounds, nor terminated by silence; how much more could this Word, this great Word.... go forth to reveal Itself to the eyes of men, and, on the other hand, illuminate the minds of the angels! And appear on earth, and, on the other hand, transcend the heavens! And be made man, and, on the other hand, make men![2]

Implications

Much of the poetry in the original Latin is lost in translation, but the power of the rhetorical structure using "contraries" comes through even in the English. We can still hear powerful passages that sound remarkably like Augustine in churches such as some African American congregations that have strong oral (rhetorical) traditions. This kind of careful structuring (including his use of "similarities") can be an excellent way of communicating difficult doctrinal ideas in a lively and interesting manner.

Augustine's emphasis on varying the styles—subdued, temperate, and grand—involving the form, content, and manner of our delivery may be instructive for us. We may resist conscious variance in style, for it may seem like congregational manipulation to us. But for him it was good communication, like giving a gift with the proper wrapping. Our purpose is not to imitate someone else's styles, but to find and use our own in order to communicate more effectively.

Augustine's lack of personal reference in his sermons is in contrast to Paul and comes to our time reinforced by

Calvin and others. Many preachers have an excellent intent in this: They do not want to draw attention away from the Word. The unintended effect today can be to place the preacher above the struggles of the parishioners.

As Bible interpreters, we would do well to follow Augustine's "primary principle": keep studying a text until we have found something that contributes to the rule of love. Most of the great preachers, and in particular Luther and Wesley who developed the direction of Augustine's thought, have been attentive to Augustine's emphasis on the primacy of God's grace in overcoming our sin. Our messages can be enhanced by remembering that we are to preach grace, founded not on anything we can do on our own, but on God's generous acts of enabling love.

If grace seems absent in a Bible text, for instance in some of the words of Jesus, we can employ what I call a resurrection hermeneutic. Since most of Jesus' words were uttered during his earthly life and were themselves pointing to the necessity of the cross, we may safely assume that even their meaning has been altered by the death and resurrection of Christ. Thus from seemingly harsh words in Luke 12 (a harshness we do not avoid in our preaching!) we can also say, for instance: that we have One who stands at watch over us to be sure we are alert and not caught unaware (vv. 35-38); that Christ is the thief who has stolen into our hearts (vv. 39-40); that Christ is peace, the only One to end inevitable human fighting (vv. 49-53); that Christ has paid the last penny of our debt (v. 59).

II.
THE MIDDLE AGES

The Authority of
the Word
as Private Text

The Middle Ages, an incredibly rich period in preaching history, are characterized by rigid adherence to the fathers of the church, in other words, to the established authority of tradition. This was already clearly stated in the West by Cassiodorus (d. 580), who urged that the fathers be considered "divine beyond doubt": "If we should happen to find anything out of harmony and inconsistent with the method of the Fathers, let us resolve that it should be avoided."[1] The writings of the fathers were at least preserved, if not studied, by the monasteries through periods of social and political turnover during and after the collapse of the Roman Empire (c. 476). Knowledge of the biblical languages was mostly lost. In fact as time wore on, Latin, never the vernacular in the North of Europe, was less and less the vernacular in the South. It continued to be the language of the mass, however, and became unintelligible even to many priests. Increasingly the Bible became the private text of a privileged few.

There were roughly two periods to the Middle Ages, each containing its own preaching revival. From 650 to around 1200, the monastic system helped provide an element of order in the harsh drudgery of European life. Monasteries had spread from the East, partly due to Chrysostom's deacon, Cassian (c. 360–435), who fled to the West when Chrysostom was banished. In 415 he established monastic communities for men and women in Marseilles along the Eastern models. Benedict founded his monastery around 529 and included reading Cassian's *Conferences* as mandatory in the *Benedictine Rule*, a book which guided monastic life in the West. In the same year the Second Council of Vaison approved a practice that already had broad common acceptance and that we saw with both Chrysostom and Augustine: Priests were formally allowed to preach in addition to bishops, and, in the absence of a priest, deacons could read a sermon of one of the church fathers.

Education in this time was primarily for the purpose of enabling devotional readings and daily offices, although some knowledge of theology was expected. Exegesis was for moral and spiritual edification. Many preachers were often mere mouthpieces for mechanical translations from sermons by the church fathers in the common language of the people.

Cassian also brought with him a further development of Origen's three senses and Jerome's "multiple senses," in the fourfold senses or meanings of Scripture that quickly became the exegetical norm: *literal* or historical (i.e., Jerusalem = the actual city); *allegorical,* concerning the church and faith (Jerusalem = the church); *moral* or tropological (Jerusalem = the human soul); and *prophetic* or anagogical, having to do with mystical, future, or final things (Jerusalem = the heavenly city). A Latin poem helped some people to remember the differences:

> The *letter* shows us what God and our fathers did;
> The *allegory* shows us where our faith is hid;

The *moral* meaning gives us rules of daily life;
The *anagogy* shows us where we end our strife.[2]

Society was highly stratified. Parish clergy who ministered to the needs of the people were considered beneath
the elite contemplatives who dwelt in the austere seclusion
of the monasteries. The highest calling was to deny oneself,
to live a godly life, and to earn thereby heavenly blessings
on behalf of the larger society. As for the common people,
it was only by the sacraments that they could hope to be
pure in the sight of God. There were widespread abuses of
clerical and monastic positions.

Under the influence of the Carolingian renaissance and
particularly Charlemagne (d. 814), more emphasis was
given to preaching as nurture. Public worship was
reformed. The Gospel or Epistle texts would be read in
worship, translated from the Latin, and exegeted, often
with the addition of a didactic pastoral message—the
early forerunner of an exegesis-application homiletical
method that would be handed down to modern times by
the Puritans. All Christians were expected to be able to
recite the Lord's Prayer and the Creed, and preachers
were instructed to preach on these and the Ten Commandments. Scholarship was revived, focused primarily
on copying ancient manuscripts and recapturing the
understandings of the fathers. Education of the clergy
was again stressed as a way of combating idleness and
ignorance. This revival was also the beginning of centuries of great religious music (i.e., the "Gregorian
chant"), poetry and hymn writing, which were the fruit of
increased monastic enthusiasm and devotion.

When the Crusades began in 1095 (partly to recapture
Palestine and partly to reunite East and West after their
split in 1054), preaching was given additional purpose: to
recruit valiant crusaders for the harsh marches to the war
zones and to raise sponsors through the selling of indul-

gences. Even listening to sermons could merit indulgence privileges! As part of the Crusades, traveling preachers would speak outdoors, often beneath some spot marked by a portable ornate preaching cross.

The second period of the Middle Ages is roughly 1200 to 1500. Several factors influenced the widespread rebirth of preaching in this era: increased urbanization and a growth of trade and commerce that followed centuries of instability; urban mercantile and scholarly demands to hear the teaching of the church; the founding of great universities to train the clergy in centers like Bologna (founded as a law school in 1088, it added theology to its curriculum in the thirteenth century), Oxford (1214), and Paris (1215); the rediscovery of classical thought, kept alive mostly through the Islamic world, including Spain, although also in Ireland; the appropriation of recent Jewish exegetical and philological methods (pioneered particularly by Gaon Sa'adia ben Joseph, 892–942); the rise of scholasticism in the universities; and the separation of theology from biblical studies.

The new interest in preaching is reflected in a sudden spurt in the number of technical homiletical manuals, books of sermon outlines, and collections of popular homiletical moral tales or exempla. Alan of Lille (1128–1202), whose *Art of Preaching* is the first of these manuals, says that preaching should be exposition, based on a text or texts in the manner of Paul, and he provides 47 sample sermons for various occasions. Preaching, he says, is the highest calling of the "perfect" Christian, preceded by developmental stages similar to Augustine's but more specifically including the scriptural texts in the spiritual development of the preacher: confession, prayer, thanksgiving, scriptural study, consultation with experts about meanings, and expounding to others. Alan defines preaching more broadly than many do today: It is what is spoken, what is written in a letter (i.e., Paul), and what is done by deed.[3]

In many of the homiletical manuals the sermon began with a **scriptural quotation,** a statement of the **theme** (*prothema* or *antethema*), and a **prayer**. What we would consider to be the actual sermon then began and included a restatement of the theme in an **introduction** *(introductio thematis)* and a **division** of the argument *(divisio thematis)*—often using rhyming key words from the theme—usually into three points with **subdivisions**. Sermons were evaluated in part by (1) the unity of focus on one main idea, (2) the manner of the division, and (3) the **proof** of the argument *(confirmatio)*. It is this point-form of preaching which has passed down to the modern day.

This is the first time that we have seen sermon form become self-conscious: In the infant and early church, rhetorical principles were the bones beneath the material, but they did not protrude out from it. Nor did they control it in a rigid way. Classical rhetoric had five canons or basic categories of laws: Invention (the discovery of arguments to use, the most important aspect of which was the study of different kinds of logical proof); Arrangement (the structuring of arguments); Style (appropriate manners of speaking, word selection, images, phrasing, etc.); Memory (how to remember a speech); and Delivery. In the Middle Ages a process that began with Pope Gregory the Great's *Pastoral Rule* (591) was completed. The primary feature of classical rhetoric (Invention) became secondary, at best. And what were secondary features of classical rhetoric (Arrangement and Style) became primary. Herein lay the seeds for yet later historical dismissal of rhetoric as mere ornament and style.

Early church fascination with number-mysticism continued. Bonaventure (1221–1274), the Franciscan scholar, rearticulated Cassian's four senses of Scripture; he found in four senses the number of the Gospels and in three senses beyond the literal (i.e., in the spiritual senses) the number of the Trinity. Robert of Basevorn (c. 1322) provides this intriguing rationale for three points in preaching: "Only three statements, or the equivalent of three, are used in the theme—either from respect to the Trinity, or because a threefold cord is not easily broken, or because this method is mostly followed by Bernard [of Clairvaux], or, as I think more likely, because it is more convenient for the set time of the sermon."[4]

The rebirth of preaching was also largely due to the rise of new religious orders of mendicant friars who practiced true piety in the vows of poverty, chastity, and obedience. They desired to model themselves on the apostles and to bring the fruits of contemplative community life to the people. Shortly after 1200, the Order of Preachers (Dominicans) and the Order of Friars Minor (Franciscans) were started as reforms of the monastic movement. Preaching moved out into the streets, byways, and churchyards (see the cover of this book). Both Orders were devoted to evangelical preaching, but the followers of Dominic, in their mission to attack heresy, from the beginning also devoted themselves to study. Even as monastic life had been dedicated to the wisdom of the Scriptures *(sapientia scripturarum)*, the emerging scholasticism was devoted to the knowledge of the Scriptures *(scientia scripturarum)*.

CHAPTER 8

Hildegard of Bingen (1098–1179)
The Word of the Spirit

This remarkable medieval woman was a writer, healer, prophet, political activist, and preacher (with church approval) in an age when women enjoyed few rights and she herself was convinced of women's inferiority. Although she was forty-three before she began to write, the volume and range of her writing exceeds that of most men of her time. Her surviving works include biographies of saints; books on cosmology, doctrine, ethics, and medicine; visionary treatises on God's ways, life's merits, and divine works; hymns, canticles, and a musical morality play; and several hundred letters, some of which contain sermons. Abbesses at this time were allowed to preach, but not at the Sunday mass. In addition to the preaching she did as founder and first abbess of the Benedictine convent at Bingen, she undertook four preaching tours in France and Germany after she was sixty, when her fame was established, preaching in a variety of settings.

The sickly tenth child of an aristocratic family, she was offered as a tithe to God and enclosed in the cell of an aristocratic contemplative when she was eight. She was Jutta's pupil, handmaiden and companion. By the time Jutta died, her hermitage had expanded, and Hildegard, at age thirty-eight, was elected abbess in her stead. She began writing reluctantly and requested that a papal theological commission test the authenticity of her visions; *Scivias* was given the pope's approval. At considerable ecclesial risk she insisted on moving the convent away from the monastery and the men, and, later in life, she vigorously opposed the actions of her benefactor, Emperor Frederick Barbarossa, when he appointed a series of antipopes.

Hildegard was born to a noble family and remained a member of the social elite, obtaining many privileges from those with influence. The fact that she was among the spiritual elite, having papal approval of her visions, gave her authority to write and preach outside the convent. She was a forerunner of many other mystic women preachers, including St. Bridget of Sweden (1302–1373, founder of the Bridgettines), and was read widely during the Reformation—she had forecast that church corruption would lead to seizure of church wealth and dissolution of the monasteries.

Homiletical Setting

The Benedictine Order, to which Hildegard belonged, adopted Cassiodorus' attitude toward the divinity of the wisdom of the church fathers: "What book of the holy Catholic Fathers is not manifestly devoted to teaching us the straight road to our Creator?"[1] Thus her vision of the Word (*Scivias* III, 4) includes the incarnate Word, the Scriptures, and the commentaries of the fathers. Monastic education was directed toward mental and spiritual saturation with the words of Scripture through the triad of prayer, perfection, and service to God. Mystical experience could be an outgrowth of this: It was understood as intuitional, as a means of apprehending reality. It was independent of the senses and reason and allowed unity with God, the source of all knowledge.

Unlike that of most mystics, Hildegard's emphasis is

doctrinal, not experiential, and is more on seeing and understanding than on feeling. As one scholar has noted: "She meditates not on the experience of . . . languishing with desire for Christ her bridegroom, but on the place of the human person . . . in a divine plan."[2] In this she was unlike St. Symeon The New Theologian (949–1022) in the East, the great preacher Bernard of Clairvaux (1090–1153) in France, and other later mystics. For her, the Old Testament is Law and the New Testament is Grace (*Scivias* 4:5). All creation forms a marvelous unity, with God and the incarnate Word at the center. "God's WORD," she says, "is in all creation, visible and invisible. The Word, is living, being, spirit, all verdant greening, all creativity. All creation is awakened, called, by the resounding melody, God's invocation of the WORD."[3] All is to work for the harmony which God has ordained through nature, the church, history, and society. All is to move toward God's purpose. Hildegard combines three elements: strong conservative doctrine, poetic visions similar to those in Revelation, and allegory and numerology.

Even as the church fathers were regarded as divine, so too were authentic visions. Hildegard's visions came to her while she was fully alert, perhaps assisted by a lifelong migraine illness. In one of these, she was told by God that she already understood the exposition of Scripture. She was to both "speak and write what you see and hear." Her visions along with Scripture became the basis of her preaching and teaching life at the convent. Like other visionaries, she describes the vision, clarifies its moral or doctrinal meaning image by image and using allegory, and finds scriptural support, again using allegory.

Sermon Sample

In this sample from a sermon at Cologne, she speaks as God's voice to the gathered clergy:

Oh my dear sons, who feed my flocks. . . . I have placed you like the sun and other luminaries that you may give light to men through the fire of teaching, shining in good report and offering burning hearts. . . . But you are prostrate and do not sustain the Church. You flee to the cavern of your delight and because of the tedium of riches and the avarice of other vanities you do not fill those under you, nor allow them to seek teaching from you. [Later, in her own voice, she warns against the Albigensians:] While they remain with you, you cannot be safe. The Church mourns and wails over their wickedness while her sons are polluted by their iniquity. Therefore cast them from yourselves, lest the community and city perish.[4]

The second sample uses what Augustine and classical rhetoric called "similarities" and "contraries." It is from a vision in which a pit with fiery stench opens to blow on a white cloud of "beautiful human form," and, as a result, "all the elements of the world, which before had existed in great calm, were turned to the greatest agitation and displayed horrible terrors." She interprets it this way:

Spirit is to be tested by spirit, flesh by flesh, earth by water, fire by cold, fight by resistance, good by evil, beauty by deformity, poverty by riches, sweetness by bitterness, health by sickness, long by short, hard by soft, height by depth, light by darkness, life by death, Paradise by punishments, the Heavenly Kingdom by Gehenna, earthly things by earthly things and heavenly things by heavenly things. Hence Man is tested by every creature, in Paradise, on earth and in Hell; and then he is placed in Heaven. You see clearly only a few things among many that are hidden from your eyes. So why do you deride what is right, plain and just, and good among all good things in the sight of God? Why do you think these things unjust? God is just, but the human race is unjust in transgressing God's precepts when it claims to be wiser than God.[5]

Implications

Hildegard's visions may lack realism. However, her preaching displays a political realism from which we can benefit. She did not verbally challenge the exclusion of women from preaching in her time, yet she dared to preach beyond her convent; when she did preach she did not play safe but used her papal sanction to attack the wrongs she saw in the priesthood. Political savvy is part of preaching, although we might wish it were not. We could try to be as wise as she is in assessing when an issue is sufficiently important to risk everything, and when it is best to walk more gently for the sake of God's ministry.

Hildegard uses the rich imagery of her visions as a text for her preaching, and she needed to, for they were not only her divine license for undertaking preaching tours, they were her distinctive message. We may find her visions curious, but she uses them in excellent fashion. She devised a method for interpreting them that allowed her to bring forth scriptural truths. If we could devise such skill in reading God's actions in just the cultural images and events surrounding us, such that we might find God's signature of love, mercy, peace, justice, and righteousness in unexpected places, our own faith and our people's faith would grow. They would begin to recognize God in their own daily lives.

Finally, we might learn from the harmony she found in all creation. The word she coined, *veriditas*, for the power of greening, can be a reminder of how much we must learn, alter our life-style, and preach about caring for the world if life on this planet is to continue as we know it.

CHAPTER 9

Thomas Aquinas (c. 1225–1274)
The Word of Reason

By the time Thomas Aquinas completed his studies at the University of Naples and decided to join the Order of Preachers in 1243, the scholastic movement was already underway. Newly rediscovered Aristotelian principles of empirical knowledge were being brought to bear by the universities on the church's past, with much opposition. The church fathers no longer served as simple self-evident "proofs" of church doctrine. Anselm of Canterbury (1033–1109) had devised a method of applying reason to support matters that were already decided by faith. Peter Abelard (1079–1142) cleverly demonstrated in *Sic et Non (Yes and No)* the contradictions amongst the church fathers. And Peter Lombard (d. 1160), whose *Four Books of Sentences* was to serve as the standard theological textbook until the Reformation, adopted Abelard's dialectical method in compiling and discussing ancient and contemporary ideas. Lombard organized them systematically under four headings: God, Created Beings, Salvation, and the Last Things.

Aquinas had been placed in a Benedictine abbey at age five with the intent that he might become an abbot. His decision at age nineteen to become a begging Dominican friar was not well received by his noble family. His brother was dispatched on the highway to France to return him home by force, where he stayed for a year. Nonetheless, he could not be dissuaded (some claim that a prostitute was once hired for the purpose). He was ordained and appointed as the doctoral student for one of the two professorships assigned to the Dominicans at Paris. As a professor (1256–59) he would have taught in the three areas of study: homiletics, commentary on Lombard's *Sentences*, and theological debate.

During the next decade of teaching in Italy, he wrote his famous *Summa theologiae*, a systematic and dialectical summary of theology; in it he moves, as did his theology classes, from *question* to *arguments against* his position to *arguments for* it. It was the classic mode of *medieval disputation*. He returned to Paris for a second term and died before he was fifty. The one who earned the nickname "dumb ox" for his early silence as a student, was the greatest theologian of his age.

The early church had tried to synthesize Greek thought and Christian truths. Aquinas now sought to reconcile the rediscovered Aristotelian philosophy with Christianity. He argued that nature and reason should be kept separate from revelation and the supernatural. Rational science, based in empirical evidence gathered by the senses, confirmed revealed knowledge about God (i.e., that God is the "first cause"), although there were some truths or mysteries, such as the Trinity and incarnation, that could not be demonstrated. Reason supports faith rather than undermines it. The four virtues that remained after the fall (prudence, courage, self-control, and justice) are adequate for reading the Scriptures and for living at least a good life. Through the gift of God's free and unmerited grace, received exclusively through the sacraments, the three Christian virtues (faith, hope, and love) are bestowed, enabling people to do acts earning merit. Grace and merit were the primary concepts of medieval piety.

Aquinas' work was a move toward openness and away

from the tyranny of the past. Although he is primarily remembered as a great systematic theologian who placed high value on reason, reason on its own could not lead to truth. Faith also was necessary. Since he regarded humans as supernatural as well as natural, the highest calling of Christians, one that could not be fully achieved in this life, was the contemplation of God. Aquinas was thus also a mystic.

Homiletical Setting

It is typical in writing the history of the church that the preaching of the great theologians has been largely ignored. It is all the more remarkable and ironic with Aquinas, who chose specifically to be in the Order of Preachers. Only in his prayers and his more than 150 sermons do we find his professed love of symbolism. The latter come to us only in point form and represent a skeletal version of clearly ordered thought. It is inconceivable that he could have preached these in their present form, though some have suggested that he did. Rather they are sermon outlines he preached and homiletical aids for students and Dominicans to transcribe and develop, in part or in whole, complete with valuable and numerous additional texts to consult, in the medieval tradition of "prepared sermons." We know that his preaching was powerful: When preaching in Naples and Rome he repeatedly moved people to tears and had to pause to allow the congregation to weep. His appeal was broad to both commoners and intellectuals.

In keeping with his own emphasis on reason, and in anticipation of Protestant ideals, Aquinas restores to primacy the literal, historical sense of Scripture. He says it is the only sense of Scripture from which one can argue, since it derives from images having to do with the body's physical senses, from which our knowledge springs. The other spiritual senses, which may be collectively categorized as allegory, are interpretations of the literal and presuppose it. Nothing is lost by use of allegory "since nothing essential to the faith is contained in the spiritual sense of one passage which is not clearly expressed in the literal sense of another."[1] As with Chrysostom, the literal sense is what the author intended, though it includes metaphorical meaning; it "cannot contain what is false." It was this latter idea which led Aquinas to insist that the Garden of Eden was fact, and led others to complain that he was too literal.

From his sermons we may observe at least three things about his particular brand of literalism: (1) Every detail in a statement he makes is supported by a particular quotation from Scripture—this is in part because he links his allegorical or symbolic readings back to other texts read literally; (2) every quotation, including the initial verse which is his text, stands on its own as a literal complete truth without support from its context; (3) his use of allegory is no less wildly symbolic than that of earlier preachers, although it is sometimes more subdued, functioning at times more as a simile than as an absolute one-to-one correspondence, detail for detail. His text, "The deep uttered his voice, and lifted up his hands on high" (Hab. 3:10), is "applied to" St. Thomas who is "deep" (for several reasons, which he names), and to Christ who "lifted up his hands" to Thomas (again for several reasons).

Aquinas' sermons provide an early example of what came to be known as "university sermons" because of their numerous and elaborate divisions (points) and subdivisions. His homiletical method, perhaps too simply stated, is this: Start with a verse from scripture; either make a number of main points (headings) from it and support these with verses from other texts, or, start by finding verses from other texts that are similar to the first one, and use them instead to make as many main points as necessary. His next step is to make subpoints in the same manner, if they are necessary, using the new or additional textual verses. He treats each point in turn, developing the idea clearly before going on to proof texts, and shapes the whole by his doctrinal understanding.

Sermon Sample

The following sermon outline is from the First Sunday in Advent on the text "The day is at hand" (Rom. 13:12). We must imagine its development. We begin with his own opening words. We depart from his single-paragraph format and mark commentary using brackets []:

This word *Day* is to be taken in a four-fold sense—"The *Day* is at hand;" the day of *mercy*, the day of *grace*, the day of *justice*, and the day of *glory*. [This represents both his **introduction** of his theme and his **division.** His first division (I: A) focuses on the word *day*, to which he brings four subdivisions, formed according to the four *senses* of Scripture and his doctrine.] That Sun makes this a four-fold day, whose advent holy Church now celebrates.

[*Subdivision i*] The day of mercy is the birth-day of the Lord [subpoint a—the literal sense], in which the Sun of Righteousness arises upon us [subpoint b—the allegorical sense]; or more truly, He Who made that day so glorious [subpoint c—developed to be either the moral sense or the prophetic sense].

[*Subdivision ii*] The day of grace is the time of grace [the allegorical sense];

[*Subdivision iii*] the day of justice is the day of judgement [the moral sense];

[Subdivision iv] the day of glory is the day of eternity [the prophetic sense].

Aquinas now goes on to quote four additional Scripture passages as authorities (proofs), one to support each point:

Joel speaks of the first—iii. 18—"In that day the mountains shall drop down new wine, and the hills shall flow with milk." Concerning the second, 2 Cor. vi. 2, "Behold, now is the day of salvation." Of the third, Wis. i.[2]

Aquinas' next division (his second division I: B) with subdivisions is: "The birth-day of the Lord draws near, that devoutly the day of *mercy* may be celebrated and honoured; the day of *grace* that it may be received; the day of *judgement* that it may be feared; the day of *glory* that it may be attained." Four additional texts are then quoted, one for each point.

The first half of his sermon is now complete. The second half is divided in two parts. In the first (II: A), Aquinas identifies the virtues appropriate to the celebration of the days of mercy (mercy and truth), grace (purity and humility), judgment (meditation and fear), and glory (righteousness). Texts are quoted for each virtue in passing. In the second (II: B), he returns to Romans to demonstrate in turn how Paul exhorts us to the virtues of mercy and truth, and to purity and humility.

Implications

Some might be tempted to judge Aquinas: for his use of proof texts and allegory; for the structure of his argument and its singular appeal to reason, to the exclusion of emotion; for his exclusion of his own and our experience; and his easy assumption of the objective truth of what he speaks. But these would be superficial and unfair responses to what is after all only an outline. In his sermons, unlike so many of his writings, we see Aquinas reaching out to the common people as well as the educated. Here we see him playing with images and ideas, promoted by the different "senses," that have emotional appeal as well as logical.

Aquinas was positioned for his age. In the same way that his *Summa contra Gentiles* was written as an aid to missionaries who had to debate with heretics, his sermon outlines were passed on to preachers needing help with a new approach to preaching provided by the scholastics. Most popular sermons of his time were appealing not to reason but to moralistic and fantastic stories (exempla), obedience, emotion, visions, and much more exaggerated use of allegory than he employs. He roots his preaching in the Bible. The closest parallel we have today is various publications that give weekly biblical ideas to preachers, e.g., *Word and Witness.* Aquinas, though a great theologian, did not see himself as above this task and made his expertise available to local preachers.

There are pleasing qualities in his preaching. One is the predictable movement of his sermons. He goes from a clearly stated idea to related sub-ideas and exegetical movements into the text. It is easy to follow what he is saying because he is so well organized. His sermon also moves from discussion of a particular doctrine to a final exhortation concerning what we might now do specifically in our own lives. Perhaps we could identify, as students of Aquinas, techniques that would help us to structure modern theological arguments.

Such techniques might be issue-centered: Start with a need in the congregation (e.g., to establish a mission for the poor); identify the underlying issue or barrier (e.g., we do not want to enter the suffering of others); clarify a doctrine that speaks to the issue (e.g., Christ has entered our suffering); point to the consequences of that truth in each of our lives (e.g., because we have experienced God meeting our needs, we are here); and move back to the original need, this time with a fresh perspective (e.g., we are stronger for entering the suffering of others for there we encounter Christ). Often, current preachers who use rich imagery are lacking an identifiable order to their thought that many listeners, less attuned to imagery, require.

Much preaching today has lost sight of discussing Aquinas' Christian virtues. Discussion of virtues may have lapsed, but such preaching could be as helpful to our people as it was to Aquinas' listeners. A sermon series on the nine fruits of the Spirit in Galatians 5:22 would develop the virtues of love, joy, peace, patience, kindness, generosity, faithfulness, gentleness, and self-control.

We might also learn from him the manner in which rich use of symbols can enhance mystery in preaching. Frederick Buechner once said that preaching should merely put a frame around the mystery. Although Aquinas uses the "senses" of Scripture, appropriate to the hermeneutic of his time, as a source of imagery, we cannot. But we can be attentive to resonant imagery that will help us "frame" the mystery, imagery in various biblical texts, literature, culture, and daily experience. Metaphor is essential for theology, and careful, somewhat restrained use of it not only contributes to a sermon being memorable, it also awakens our imagination to the possibilities of the faith. Aquinas used one image, the Day at hand, as the controlling image by repeating it and exploring it from a number of angles. Preached just prior to the longest night of the year, this sermon would provide a powerful theological image for his congregation through the week.

III.
THE REFORMATIONS

The Authority of
the Common Text

The Reformation is a distinct period in history that begins after the year 1500, and we may think of the time since then as the period of the continuing reformations. The challenges to the absolute authority of the church, and the Protestant emphases on direct individual relationships with God, on common access to Scripture, and on individual joyful witness to God (the reason Reformers called themselves "evangelical"), has meant successive "revolutions." Each age has seen new sects and denominations form as individuals and groups reassess their relationship to God and society.

The Reformation's roots extend much farther than the sixteenth century into history. We have seen that following the collapse of the Roman Empire, and with it the collapse of many political institutions and functions, the one European institution which remained intact was the church. It stepped into the vacuum and took over many governmental functions, and thereby opened itself to corruptions that the Gregorian movement sought to reform in the eleventh and twelfth centuries. Austere priestly life and a unified society dominated by the church and its leaders were the Gregorian ideals. The ideals survived, even though the reform movement did not, and they survived in different ways: in the mendicant orders of friars; in a wide variety of new groups and orders across Europe; and in sects like the Hussites in Bohemia, the Lollards, followers of John Wycliffe, in England, and numerous others particularly in France and Italy.

Many of the Reformation ideas to purify the church morally and doctrinally had been in the air for some time. The Waldensians had been against the use of Latin. The Hussites had insisted that the laity be given communion in two elements, not just bread. Many people anticipated Luther by pressing questions about the propriety of selling indulgences. In fact Erasmus found nothing heretical in Luther's attack against them. People like Erasmus had appealed to reason and the ethical teachings of Christ to reform both church and society. Some, like John Wycliffe (c. 1329–1384), had called for a return to the authority of Scripture alone in interpreting Scripture, and in deciding matters of religious duty, faith, and ecclesiastical order. He also began translating the Bible into English. And Aquinas had already turned many minds back to the primacy of the literal interpretation.

The Reformation succeeded, quite apart from its leadership, because ecclesial and political discontent was widespread. Luther's own assessment of his unique contribution was that where others criticized the life of the church (the practice), he attacked the doctrine (the theory).

Discontent at that time was widespread, and change was often adopted as much for political or pragmatic reasons as for theological or ideological ones. Divisions were often cemented by leaders unable to agree on specific doctrinal points. For instance, Luther, Zwingli, and Calvin were in agreement on the centrality of the Word. They agreed that the sacraments must be accompanied by the proclamation of the Word. (They did not say the converse, that the Word must in all cases be accompanied by the sacrament; the normal Reformed service through the week, if not on Sunday, was a service of the Word without Table.) And they agreed that the priest's words did not physically change the bread and wine. But Luther nonetheless maintained the literal truth of Christ's words, "This is my body," against Zwingli, who read that the same words merely "signify" Christ's spiritual presence. Calvin took a compromise position in claiming Christ's real presence in the elements as a mystery.

The preachers in this period appeal to different sources of authority in addition to Scripture. Scriptural texts were now in the common language and published, no longer private in the possession of a few. The idea of authoritative interpretation was severely challenged. Once central absolute authority was abandoned, reformations spread like widening ripples on a disturbed pond. Luther did not initially intend to separate from the Roman Catholic Church. Similarly, the early Methodists did not plan to separate from the Anglicans, the early Salvation Army did not plan to separate from the Methodists, and the early Pentecostals did not plan to separate from their denominations that included the Methodists. New authorities or paradigms are constantly found in history to legitimate both traditional and innovative expressions of the faith.

The Reformation also contributed to the Enlightenment of the seventeenth and eighteenth centuries. Not all of the new authorities and paradigms led toward the Christian faith. One of the new paradigms that led away from the faith was *right reason*, adopted from Aristotle and others by the Deists: By proper use of reason, one could discover universal principles of natural religion. These rationalist principles allowed for a God who was the first cause and grand Architect of all, but Deists rejected grand metaphysical theories that had no basis in empirical evidence. Thus Deists like Voltaire, Hermann Reimarus, and even more radical David Hume rejected Scripture, revelation, miracles, the Incarnation, and the Trinity. Unitarian congregations benefited from the Deist influence in churches, and many prominent preachers remaining in Trinitarian denominations were led to embrace an intellectual, emotionally cool, rationalist faith.

Another paradigm or authority, *the scientific method*, similarly pushed away from the church. This method of acquiring knowledge, whether by induction (Francis Bacon) or deduction (Descartes), was based in practical experiment and empirical evidence gathered and analyzed independent of the moral teachings of the church. Thus Galileo was condemned before the Inquisition for confirming Copernicus' claim that the planets revolve around the sun. Thus Newton explained the universe in terms of gravity. And thus eventually theology was deposed as "queen of the sciences" and science was separated from theology. History came to be understood not simply as the account of salvation of human souls. Books like Bacon's *New Atlantis* and More's *Utopia* helped envision a future ideal society on earth that humanity could shape and develop. The idea of progress was born alongside the industrial revolution, and with it the eventual idea that nature was there not to impart divine lessons but to be conquered by humans.

A third paradigm contributed to the complex developments of this period and emerged in reaction to Aristotelean classicism, rationalism, and scientific progress. It was the paradigm of *feelings and emotions*, particularly as the necessary complement to reason in a hierarchy of human psychological "faculties." Its early public religious expression was the heartfelt experience of John Wesley in 1738 and the First Great Awakening in New England in 1740. Later it would result in the Romantic movement with its rejection of classical forms and values and its revaluing of nature, organic form in art, and imagination as the highest form of reason.

As we move through this period of reformations a number of themes will emerge. These include the frequent recurrence of law and gospel as the primary theological-homiletical motifs; the adoption of cultural progress as a theological norm; the elevation of the individual in Protestant thought; a movement away from the rigidity of allegory (which insists on comparative similarity in all respects) toward analogy (which invites similarity in only some respects); and the evolution of metaphor from being a figure of speech to being one model of thought.

One theme that does not emerge as clearly as we might expect is increased attention to the biblical text. Luther and Calvin, whose extensive writing of biblical commentaries frequently had direct impact on their preaching, assume the sentence as the unit of meaning, not the individual word in the manner of the early church. And perhaps because many of their sermons are exegetical, they often locate the biblical sentence in its textual context. But most of these preachers, most of the time, show little concern in their sermons for what we identify as an opening up of the biblical text or for developments occurring in biblical studies (for instance the growing awareness of the historical framework of the Scriptures). We see glimpses of critical work in Bushnell or in James S. Stewart, who himself became a New Testament professor at the end of a long preaching career. But our own, modern preaching emphasis on the sentence in context, which almost expands the unit of meaning from the sentence to the pericope, for the most part is absent.

CHAPTER 10

Martin Luther (1483–1546)
Lutheran Protestant—the Authority of Law and Gospel

Martin Luther was a brilliant Augustinian monk whose discipline of piety and good works led him more and more to question a basic medieval concept, the link between good works and God's grace. Luther was tormented with a guilty conscience. In the daily sacrament of confession, he was never sure that he had confessed all of his sins, motives, and repressed thoughts. If he had not, how could he be absolved? He had a debilitating sense that he was lost, that his own efforts would never be adequate for God. Eventually the "righteousness of God" in Romans 1:17 ceased exclusively to mean for him the measuring scales by which God judges us, as his teachers had told him. Rather it was also what God works in us when we call out to God. We are saved by grace alone *(sola gratia)* and by faith alone *(sola fide)* through no works or merit of our own. This was to be for him a new theological paradigm. It contributed to the most widespread reforms and divisions in the history of the church.

By the time Luther came to this new belief, he was a professor at Wittenberg, a humble university in a humble German town. Several years earlier he had broken with the wishes of his working class parents, who had hoped he would enter law. He had been entrusted by his Order to journey to Rome on a matter that required a direct appeal. The journey was long and proved fruitless. On his return, he accepted the Rome verdict against the appeal, a move that did not please his colleagues. He was forced to leave the relative prestige of the University of Erfurt.

Disputes and conflicts would mark his life to the end. His Ninety-five Theses, nailed to the cathedral door, were against a preaching tour that had come to the area. The tour was selling indulgences to help build the Sistine Chapel, and unfortunately for Luther, it was sanctioned by Rome. Luther argued that indulgences offered salvation for cash, without any demands for a penitent heart. Printing presses, newly invented, were unhindered by copyright (a forthcoming policy of the Church of England to protect intellectual property from commercial presses) and quickly translated and circulated Luther's text.

The chain reaction he started surprised him. It was fueled by popular national sentiments against foreign jurisdictions siphoning tax funds away from the region. Soon Luther needed the protection offered by Frederick III, Elector of Saxony. He appealed unsuccessfully for a "reasoned," "scriptural" explanation of his error from Rome. As the conflict dragged on, Luther continued to study, preach, and publish, intensifying his criticisms of some established doctrines of the church. Finally he denied the supreme authority of the pope. At the Diet of Worms in 1521, he was summoned to recant his published views. He restated his understanding that Scripture was to be interpreted by the authority of Scripture alone (sola Scriptura), and not by unwritten oral tradition. Then he added his famous words, "Here I stand. I can do no other. God help me! Amen." He was placed under imperial ban and for ten months was given protective custody at Wartburg Castle, during which time he translated the New Testament for the first time into German (using Erasmus's Greek-Latin text). At this time he also wrote the *Church Postil* (also called his *Wartburg Postil*, vol. 52 of his *Works*) for preachers, which he identified as "the very best book which I ever wrote."

He had been teaching that the priesthood and celibacy were not means of receiving grace and that priests who wanted to marry should do so. He took his own advice in 1525 and subsequently had six children with Katharina von Bora, a former nun. He continued to preach several times a week as well as to write and teach. By the time of his death in 1546, the Reformation had spread across Europe; he had translated the entire Bible; published more than 400 pamphlets and books, 37 hymns, and 2,300 sermons (transcribed by others) and postils. The latter include his beloved *Church Postil*, which provided ministers with sermon guides, exegetical material, and sermons he may not have actually preached that were written for the use of other ministers. He had also organized a new church with a revised liturgy and new system of government. His close colleague Melanchthon quoted Erasmus in the funeral sermon: The magnitude of the disorders demanded God send "a violent physician."

Homiletical Setting

Luther's key insight is that God's work makes us righteous, not our own, and thus it is by our faith alone, in response to God's work, that we are saved. This insight changed his reading of Scripture and encouraged him to speak of law and gospel. By using Scripture to verify one's righteousness, as he saw others doing, one brought judgment upon oneself. The purpose of the law was utterly to destroy any pretensions we might have about our own ability to be righteous. Only when we have cast ourselves entirely upon God's mercy are we able to receive the gospel and the truth that God's saving grace is freely given.

There were several implications for preaching: (1) Law and gospel exist beside each other in the Scriptures; thus for instance the first commandment stands at once as a statement both of condemnation (i.e., you are not to have other gods) and of salvation (i.e., you may put your entire trust in me). (2) Using a play on the word *Spiegel*, he sees law as both God's judgment and a mirror in which we see ourselves unmasked. (3) Law and gospel are determined partly by the manner in which we receive them. (4) Law points to the necessity of Christ. Gospel points to the consolation in Christ that God offers all. (5) The primary responsibility of the church is preaching. It is to ensure that both law and gospel will be heard for salvation.

Erasmus argued that reading and reason were sufficient for understanding the Bible, but for Luther the Holy Spirit was necessary as well. Scripture becomes the Word of God only when it is read and correctly interpreted. Scripture is to be explained by other, clearer scripture. The gospel, or Good News of Christ, by its nature is oral. It is both message and event here and now. As it was for the early church, it exists as an event in sound, not as written document. This Word calls the church into being. As he said, in characteristic style, the gospel "should not be written but shouted"; the church "is not a pen-house but a mouth house."[1]

Some other homiletical principles may be briefly identified: He is christocentric in his reading of all Scripture; he employs only two senses of Scripture, the literal (i.e., the natural meaning it has through history) and the allegorical (generally used to provide a christological reading for the Old Testament). Sermons are to focus on a biblical text; his exegetical sermons, for instance his three volumes of sermons on the Gospel of John, stay with the text verse by verse. Sermons are to speak to the heart of the listeners "as simply and as childishly and as popularly and as commonly" as possible.[2] Luther's approach, particularly after 1521, is usually exegetical or thematic with no formal introductions, divisions, or conclusions. Often topics begun on one day are carried forward in his preaching on the next occasion. His churches had morning and evening services of the Word each weekday in addition to the Sunday services.

Sermon Sample

The following sermon, "On the Sum of the Christian Life," was preached in 1532 to German royalty who had just introduced the Reformation to their territories:

For the Scriptures teach me that God established two seats for men, a judgment seat for those who are still secure and proud and will neither acknowledge nor confess their sin, and a mercy seat for those whose conscience is poor and needy, who feel and confess their sin, dread his judgment, and yearn for his grace. . . . Consequently we must now learn to distinguish between the two parts which are called the law and the gospel, which is something that we are always teaching. The law brings us before the judgement seat, for it demands that we must be good and love out of a pure heart and a good conscience. . . . The law keeps harrying you and accusing you through your own conscience, which testifies against you . . . and there is not help or counsel for you unless you know that you can flee from the judgment seat to the mercy seat. . . . But we teach that one should know and look upon Christ as the one who sits there as the advocate of the poor, terrified conscience, believe in him, not as a judge, who is angry and ready to punish, but as a gracious, kindly, comforting mediator between my fearful conscience and God, and says to me: If you are a sinner and are terrified, and the devil is drawing you to the judgment seat through the law, then come unto me and have no fear of any wrath. . . . Thus through faith we are made wholly safe and secure, so that we shall not be condemned, not because of our holiness or purity, but because of Christ . . . sure that in and with him no wrath can remain, but only love, pardon, and forgiveness. . . . For, after all, everyone must realize that Christ and his work is not my work and life, but separated from the law and all men's work.[3]

Implications

Many of Luther's sermons continue to have remarkable vitality. He normally preached to the common, ordinary people, using vernacular, earthy language. (He says in one sermon, "Even a sow could be a [bad] Christian, for she has a big enough snout to receive the sacraments outwardly.")[4] His high doctrine of the Word, which elevates proclamation above all other action (at the expense, for instance, of what we would call social action), means, on the positive side, that he takes the necessary time to ensure that the gospel is heard, understood, and appropriated. There is no mistaking the consolation of Christ that he offers in the sermon just quoted.

The reason for Luther's vitality is twofold: (1) He is constantly rethinking doctrine in relation to the practice of Christian worship, life, and faith. If we were more deliberate about rethinking and articulating why we do what we do as Christians, our sermons might be heavily doctrinal, but they might also be understood as practical, having immediate relevance. (2) There is a sense of urgency in his emphasis on the individual's relationship with God.

The best homiletical tool Luther gives us is the distinction between law and gospel. We might use it to define the overall movement of the sermon, from law to gospel (if only because in the time we have for preaching, which is less than Luther's hour, there is not opportunity for a sustained development of either if there is a frequent movement back and forth). His understanding has problems: He can be understood to see law as Old Testament (when it is in both Testaments) and gospel as New Testament. Nonetheless, his distinction can help us to avoid preaching that puts all the responsibility for action upon us. Gospel focuses on God's action, and how we are enabled to do what is required by the law. Our method, which I have discussed elsewhere, can be first to struggle with a text to convict us of sin, and then, in the second half of the sermon, to allow sufficient opportunity from the text for the Spirit to give life.[5]

Many preachers were taught a method for preaching that was basically exegesis followed by an application. The trouble with this single homiletical movement into the text is that we can only emerge with law (i.e., unless we preach cheap grace that takes no account of the cross). It is better to think of the sermon, at minimum, as a twofold movement into the text, each with exegesis and application, the first time to develop law, and the second to develop gospel. By the end, the gospel does not cancel the law but stands in tension with it.

Luther spoke of an "unpreached" God, an abstract, hidden, remote, passive God who refuses to become flesh and known. In preaching, God becomes known. We might check the language we use about God to ensure that the passivity of the "unpreached" God is not carried over into the "preached" God.[6] Quite simply, we do not need a passive, couch-potato God who might know our pain, understand our suffering, hear our cries, but do nothing about them. The God we preach intercedes in history and does not avoid involvement in our lives.

CHAPTER 11

John Calvin (1509–1564)
Reformed Protestant—the Authority of Correction

Lutheranism was the pioneer expression of the Protestant Reformation. There were three other types of Protestantism in the sixteenth century: the Reformed (including the Presbyterian), the Anglican, and the radical Protestant (Anabaptist) movement of people like Thomas Müntzer, who advocated violence, or Conrad Grebel of the Brethren, or Menno Simmons who founded the Mennonites on peace. Reformed theology, in contrast to Lutheran, is more influenced by humanism and economic reform and held some hope that, if properly ordered, human society might conform with God's will. Zwingli in Switzerland was an early originator of this movement, and Calvin later became its chief proponent.

Calvin's mother died when he was young and he was reared by his father, a lawyer. He studied theology, ancient languages, literature; and he received his doctorate in law. When he fled Paris in 1534, under the charges of holding to Lutheran heresy, he resigned the church posts that gave him funding. In Switzerland at age twenty-seven, he published his first edition of the most important book of the Reformation, *The Institutes of the Christian Religion*, in which he presented doctrines largely unexplored from what was now being called "Protestant" perspective. The Bible, Augustine, and Luther were his primary sources. Over his lifetime this book would expand from six chapters to eighty.

Guillaume Farel, a fiery reform preacher, persuaded Calvin, with his exceptional legal and theological background, to stay in Geneva. Religious, educational, and political life were in need of restructuring because the Roman Catholics had been expelled in 1535. Opposition to Calvin's strict reform proposals brought about his exile in Strasbourg for three years. There he met the Lutheran Reformer Martin Bucer and married Idelette de Bure, a widow with two children. When his political party returned to power in Geneva, Calvin returned and introduced tight reforms to bring church and state into partnership. The aim was to make Geneva a model community. Immoral practices (adultery, dancing, gambling, excessive drinking, and so on) were strictly forbidden. Attendance at religious services was compulsory. Calvin insisted that the church alone have the authority to excommunicate, which in effect meant that the church determined who lived in Geneva.

There were four offices of Calvin's church: pastors, theological teachers, elders (who reported all aspects of individual moral and social life), and deacons (who cared for the poor and sick). Governing council members and ministers were chosen by election. Business, industry, banking (with fair interest), education (with particular importance given to education for ministry), and hard work were all encouraged in what some have seen as an early expression of capitalism and democracy. Calvin showed great compassion for refugees and great intolerance for heretics. He and his wife, who was ill for most of their nine years of marriage before her death, had one child of their own, who died in infancy.

The school Calvin started in 1559 was to become the

University of Geneva and the primary Reformed seminary of Europe and Great Britain. His influence includes the Scottish Presbyterians (the lowlands of Scotland had been converted by Calvinists prior to John Knox returning from Geneva in the late 1550s), Presbyterians in Hungary and elsewhere, the Puritans, the French Huguenots, and various Reformed church denominations.

Homiletical Setting

Calvin was elected pastor in 1536. After his return to Geneva in 1541, he often preached daily. More than 2,000 of his sermons survive, most from transcriptions made by a secretary.

There were many understandings common among the Reformers: justification by faith, the sole authority of Scripture, the centrality of preaching, direct personal relationships with God, and joyful individual witness to God.

Calvin's theology of the Word was without Luther's emphasis on law and gospel. He did not experience Luther's tenacious guilt. For him, the elect can be assured that they are indeed the elect, (1) by profession of faith, (2) by disciplined life, and (3) by love of the sacrament of the Lord's Supper. He replaced emphasis on the comfort of grace with the demands of grace. We are wholly without grace on our own. Through the Holy Spirit we are regenerated into a new spiritual nature that allows us to live by grace, although we continue to depend on God for our righteousness. *Edification, reproof, correction,* and *instruction* are his primary homiletical thrusts, for these enable regeneration to take place. The church is the gathering of the elect, not Luther's gathering of those who seek consolation. In Calvin's sermons, God is pictured as a strict and stern parent who punishes out of love.

Whether he is preaching exegetically or thematically, he

frequently exhorts the congregation in order that a resistant will might be changed. T. H. L. Parker identified the common pattern of Calvin's sermons to be: prayer; review of the previous sermon; two or more movements into the text, each followed by application and "exhortation to obedience"; and a final summary as a bid to pray.[1] In fact, frequently this pattern is not easy to detect, if it is present. Formal divisions are often few.

His liturgy was similar to Luther's. Luther retained the medieval lectionary system whereby a range of biblical texts were to be read in a certain period of the Christian year. Calvin, following Zwingli, rejected it along with the observance of a church year, including Christmas and Easter (with a few exceptions). Although he favored weekly communion, as opposed to the annual communion of the medieval Roman Catholic Church, his 1541 proposal for monthly celebration (following the Lutherans in Strasbourg) was rejected by the Genevan Council in favor of a quarterly service. The service of the Word, otherwise known as the ante-communion service, came to dominate, with the sermon as its focus. His general preaching pattern was to work through the Bible, book by book, preaching without notes, using the extensive commentaries he was writing to provide background material for his preaching. He preached daily on the weekdays of alternate weeks, for which he used the Old Testament. On Sundays he preached twice, using New Testament texts in the morning, often harmonizing the Gospels, and the Psalms later in the day.

Calvin's church was intolerant of art in the sanctuary, including vestments. The cross in Calvin's church was bare. Where Luther encouraged poets to write hymns in the everyday language for the congregation to sing, Calvin emphasized singing particularly the psalms (hence, from the Presbyterians, the Scottish Psalter). Where Luther was fiery in his manner and subject of address, Calvin was often cool and intellectual.

Calvin helped to lay the foundations for modern biblical criticism and preaching, employing several humanist principles from Erasmus and others. William J. Bouwsma notes that Calvin recognized the hand of editors in the transmission of biblical texts, and saw errors in some (e.g., the star in Matthew must have been a comet). He made allowances for some texts on the basis of historical time and culture. He read ancient authorities (i.e., church fathers) not as vehicles of transcendent knowledge but as human beings with purposes behind their words. He understood biblical texts to be acts of interpretation in themselves. Knowledge of biblical rhetoric allowed him to embrace not only the literal or "natural sense" of scripture, but also the various senses implied by ancient figures of speech. Finally, he tried to understand scriptural ideas within their context, as part of a whole.

For all of his attention to exegetical details of the text, in his commentaries as well as his sermons, Calvin often supplies reasons for actions that are not in the text itself. (Augustine had justified doing this if the motive was love.) Because of his belief (with Paul) that all Scripture is profitable for doctrine, he finds a moral where often there is none. He tends to judge the biblical characters rather than sympathize with them; thus he dismisses Job's longing for death as "inexcusable excess."[2]

Sermon Sample

Calvin's sermon, "The Proper Use of Scripture," has within it a prescription for preaching. It is based on II Timothy 3:16-17 ("All scripture . . . is profitable for doctrine, for reproof, for correction, for instruction in righteousness . . .'"):

When the Word of God is rightly expounded, the faithful are not only edified, but if an unbeliever come into the church and hear the doctrine of God he is reproved and judged. . . .

. . . our hearts are in darkness. What then must we do? We must apply the Word of God to our use, and be awakened out of sleep: we must no more forget God, nor the salvation of our own souls; we must search the very depth of our hearts, and examine our whole lives; that we may be ashamed of our filthiness, and become our own judges, to avoid the condemnation that is ready at the hand of God. Thus we understand what St. Paul meaneth by the word *reproof.*

It is not enough for men to lay the blessings of God before us, and say, this is God's will; but we must be awakened to think upon it in good earnest, and look narrowly to ourselves: yea, and to draw near to God, as if He had summoned us to appear before His judgment seat: we must bring all to light, that we may be ashamed of our evil deeds: and when we breathe into this heavenly air we must be careful not to turn aside from the right way.

It is not enough to be thus *reproved,* but *correction* must be added likewise: we must be chastised, as it were, by the Word of God, to the end that we may be reformed. We must forsake our sins; we must be sharply dealt with, that they may be plucked out by the roots, and separated from us. Thus, when we have been roused to think upon God, we feel condemned before Him, while our sins are laid open to view; and we become guilty in the sight of both God and man. Moreover, we must be drawn to it by force; if we have been drunk with delicacies, if we have indulged ourselves in folly and vanity, and have thereby been deceived, the corrections must be quick and severe, that we may give God the honor, and suffer Him to reform us, and bring us into subjection to His will.[3]

Implications

Calvin was not against art; he was against religious images in churches. His sermons contain rich imagery, though lean and controlled. In the passage just given, we can experience the effect of using one controlling image throughout. It is the image of a sinner being awakened after a night of drunkenness.

A strength of Calvin's preaching, in addition to his simplicity of imagery and the clarity of his step-by-step doctrine, is the importance he gives to exhortation. He does not assume that hearing the truth is enough: A stubborn will must be persuaded. This exhortation is as much for the encouragement of the elect, that they may continue their faithful journey, as it is for the unbeliever. In our own preaching we do well to assume that both believers and non-believers are present, and occasionally to exhort, leaving in no doubt the expectation of action.

We might also learn from the stern tone of Calvin's message. The number of times he uses "must," in the passage quoted, contributes to this. In the paragraph that immediately follows our extract, Calvin goes on to picture God as a strict parent whose love is best shown through discipline. As a result, our works are given perhaps too much emphasis, in spite of Calvin's affirmation of God's grace. The effect of these imperatives might be quite different had we lived in his Geneva and shared the urgency of a common vision of an ideal society in the making. Living as we do, in a culture which is largely suspicious of authority, Calvin's words may sound to us more authoritarian than loving, as much reflecting his legal background as his theological.

Augustine said the purpose of preaching was to delight, to persuade, and to instruct. A measure of delight or pleasure is present, at least insofar as the argument itself is pleasing. But there is little of Luther's use of humor. Emotion, color, and imagination are restrained.

Calvin's homiletic seems austere with its emphasis on edification, reproof, correction, and instruction. We would do well, however, to be instructed by his emphasis, in contrast to Luther, on social improvement. He took seriously the function of word and sacrament in creating God's realm here and now. Our own tendency to focus on individual faith and personal salvation, considered as separate from the well-being of the entire community or commonwealth, would have been foreign to him. Salvation includes being saved from our misconceptions of self, ambition, material wealth, and cultural bias and being restored to our intended purpose in God's Covenant community, as William K. McElvaney has frequently underscored for preaching.[4] In today's busy world, with fewer opportunities for members of churches to get together, there is even greater emphasis on the sermon (and a comparatively short sermon form at that!) to help shape the kind of community we are to become. We do this best when we include the concerns of individuals in the world community in our sermons. A God who in our preaching is only concerned with our local community or our region or even our own nation, is too small a God to be of relevance for most of God's children. Ultimately, of course, a God who is unconcerned for the woman who cannot feed her children in Ethiopia, cannot be counted upon to care for the needs in our midst.

CHAPTER 12

John Donne (1572–1631)
Anglican Protestant—the Authority of Metaphysical Hope

The Reformation proceeded along a simultaneous course in England, where the foundations had been laid by Wycliffe and others and where the immediate motivation was political. To facilitate his divorce and remarriage, Henry VIII established the Church of England with the king as supreme head in 1534. Protestant ideals were implemented particularly under his heir, Edward VI, who published two editions of a liturgy in English, the *Book of Common Prayer.*

The Council of Trent began in 1545 and resulted in strict ethical reform and enforcement of doctrine in the Roman Catholic Church. After England was briefly returned to Roman Catholicism under Mary, a national church was again established by Elizabeth (reign 1558–1603) under the Act of Supremacy. It was intended that it unite all the land under modest, generally Protestant ideals and an episcopal structure. Weekly and holy day attendance at church was compulsory under threat of fine. English Puritans, who wanted the Reformation to go farther, and Roman Catholics, who wanted it rolled back, persisted under persecution within the national church as well as in exile.

John Donne was born in London of Roman Catholic parents in 1572 (the same year that the Presbyterian Reformer, John Knox, died in Scotland). He studied at Oxford and Cambridge, but as a Catholic was not allowed to receive a degree. He led something of a wild life while he studied law at Lincoln's Inn, London. Among other things he went regularly to the blossoming Elizabethan theaters, including the Globe, to see Shakespeare. He became known as a poet and at some point joined the Church of England. After a time as an adventurer in naval service and then as trusted secretary of the keeper of the great seal, he was briefly thrown in prison. He had violated canon law by secretly marrying Anne More, a woman much above him in social rank, against her father's wishes. Unable thereafter to secure state employment, he and his new family were dependent upon wealthy patrons of the arts.

He did manage to win the attention of King James I, who promised him advancement if only he would seek a career in the church. He completed his theological studies with his *Essayes in Divinity*, lay-sermons on Genesis and Exodus. Finally he accepted. He was ordained in 1615 at age forty-two and thereafter wrote mainly prose. He became a royal chaplain, a famous preacher, and for the decade prior to his death in 1631 was dean of St. Paul's Cathedral. Many years earlier Anne had died, as had six of their twelve children. As a preacher he was rivaled only by Bishop Lancelot Andrewes (1555–1626).

Homiletical Setting

Donne's 160 lengthy sermons occupy ten modern volumes. He published few during his lifetime and reconstructed more than 100 of them from notes while in shelter, first from the plague (1625) and then recovering from illness (1630). In addition, his brilliant *Devotions Upon Emergent Occasions* (1624), written while recovering from relapsing fever, is a collection of short sermons for the home (like radio sermons in our time) and makes stunning and poised use of the English language and sermonic form.

Donne's mature homiletic should be understood within the Elizabethan world view. This is figuratively represented by the chain of being, which linked by analogy the world of change (i.e., nature and form) with the world of the eternal (i.e., the heavens above the moon: grace and matter). The chain moves up from mass, to vegetable, to animal, to human, to Spirit. Personality was accounted for by humors, combinations of the four basic elements (earth, air, wind, fire) and the four basic senses (hot, cold, wet, and dry). The human soul had various ascending faculties—sense, reason, and understanding—that together allowed for an understanding of God and the angels. This world view is not based in allegory.

Beauty and art were a means of assisting knowledge of God. The "metaphysical" poets were known for the breadth of their subject matter (including theology), for their wit and cleverness with images, and for their appeal to the intellect over emotion. The term has also been applied to preachers of the time with less distinctiveness (Horton Davies identifies more than forty such preachers).[1] In general they again use striking imagery from diverse sources, paradoxes, puns, and forced contrasts to arrest the imagination. In contrast to Calvin, the importance of delight is high, as is stressed in contemporary manuals such as John Hoskin's influential *Directions for Speech and Style* (1599). Donne and others like John Bunyan (1628–1688) are important in the connection of art with the English-speaking pulpit.

Donne moves the congregation to hope, even as Luther moved to gospel. As Donne said, "We preach a Kingdome, as [such] we banish from thence, all imaginary fatality" (*The Sermons of John Donne,* VIII, 165). We "preach consolation, preach peace, preach mercy." Donne organizes his sermons to move for instance from pre-death to afterlife, or from "problematical" to "dogmatical," or from life without faith to life with faith. Frequently he moves up the chain of being in various ways: from the senses to reason to understanding, from past to present to future, from memory to understanding to will for change, or from meditation about life's toils to expostulation about God's truth to prayer (see especially his *Devotions*), or from one paradox to another paradox to resolution.

As a means of developing this hope, Donne's interpretation is often sophisticated. For instance he uses a principle he calls "inverting the Text": Thus he changes Martha's, "Lord if thou hadst been here . . .," into our joyful, "Lord, because thou wast here, our Brother is not dead."[2]

Typically, in a Donne sermon, a long introduction *(proem)* is followed by a formal discussion of usually two or three divisions (*divisio,* i.e., main points), followed by the proof, often with numerous subdivisions in the manner of scholastic preaching. In both elaborate structure and imagery, the metaphysical preaching contrasts the Puritan "plain style."

His early biographer described Donne's weekly rhythm: "After his Sermon he never gave his eyes rest, till he had chosen out a new Text, and that night cast his Sermon into a form, and his Text into divisions; and the next day betook himself to consult the Fathers, and so commit his meditations to his memory, which was excellent."[3]

Desire to accommodate both Protestant and Roman Catholic ideas contributed to four features of the period's English homiletics: (1) use of Latin quotations, with translation; (2) appeal to the creeds, councils, and the fathers of the first five centuries; (3) a renewed interest in early church types and allegory; and (4) retaining the sermon in liturgical relationship to the Table.

Donne's use of allegory (which John Bunyan would use with little restraint), differs from that of the early church because: (1) church fathers are cited not as divine proofs but as interpreters with differences among themselves (see VIII, 41, 206); (2) allegorical readings are often offered as interpretations in need of their own rational support (see his intriguing reason for saying that Moses demanded to see Christ—VIII, 133-53, esp. 152-53); (3) with the spread of medieval notions of the analogy of being, analogy and simile become assumed ways of speaking; and (4) allegory is understood as part of the creative license of the preacher. As C. S. Lewis argued in *The Allegory of Love* (1936), the age had a long tradition of allegory in court poetry and understood it to be symbolic or metaphoric, not literal. Donne identified God as a *"literall God"* and *"a figurative, a metaphoricall God too"*; that is, God uses metaphors, allegories, hyperboles, and rhetoric: "How much oftner doth he exhibit a *Metaphoricall Christ* [i.e., the way, light, a gate, vine, bread], than a *reall*, a *literall*?"[4]

Donne's "Why Puritans Make Long Sermons" (see the epigraph of this book) was written before he became a preacher, he himself preaching the long sermons customary of the time.

Sermon Sample

From the seventeenth of Donne's *Devotions* we find this famous passage:

No Man is an *Iland*, intire of it selfe; every man is a peece of the *Continent*, a part of the *maine*; if a *Clod* bee washed away by the *Sea*, *Europe* is the lesse, as well as if a *Promontorie* were, as well as if a *Mannor* of thy *friends,* or of *thine owne* were; Any Mans *death* diminishes *me,* because I am involved in *Mankinde;* And therefore never send to know for whom the *bell* tolls: It tolls for *thee.*[5]

An excerpt from his regular liturgical preaching gives a typical use of imagery:

Here, in the *prayers* of the Congregation God comes to us; here, in his Ordinance of *Preaching,* God delivers himselfe to us; here in the administration of his *Sacraments,* he seals, ratifies, confirmes all unto us. . . . And therefore, as the *Needle* of a *Sea-compasse,* though it shake long, yet will rest at last, and though it do not look directly, exactly to the North Pole, but have some variation, yet, for all that *variation,* will rest, so, though thy heart have some variations, some deviations, some aberrations from that direct point, upon which it should be bent, which is an absolute conformity of thy will to the will of God, yet, though thou lack something of that, afford thy soul rest: settle thy soule in such an *infallibility,* as this condition can admit, and beleeve, that God receives glory as well in thy *Repentance,* as in thine *Innocence,* and that the mercy of God in Christ, is as good a pillow to rest thy soule upon *after* a sinne, as the *grace* of God in Christ is a shield, and protection for thy soule, before.[6]

Implications

Donne had been lying in illness listening to the church bells tolling the deaths in the community, wondering who had died. He used this simple bell image from common, everyday experience to such effect that the tolling bells would now remind the hearer of Donne's words. It is such simple, poignant images of the world about us that we might seek to isolate in our own sermons to imaginative effect. If Donne were to write today, he might have written about the telephone ringing, or the telegram, or the police coming to knock on the door, or perhaps the hearse driving by in the street.

The careful selection of words, the attention given to visual detail, and the balanced musical phrases Donne uses are not just a mark of metaphysical poets and preachers, they are a mark of fine rhetorical use of language to capture attention and to communicate effectively. We can enhance our own sensitivity to excellent use of language by reading fine poetry and prose (e.g., novels, biographies, book and film reviews) and by jotting down memorable phrases in our notebooks for later imitation or quotation. Doing this exercise a few times a week can make a big contribution to our preaching in the long run.

It is not surprising, given the amount of death in Donne's personal life and times, that death is a common subject of his sermons. (In fact, Donne installed his own coffin in his bedroom during his mature life and occasionally slept in it as a reminder of his mortality and of the life of sin he had renounced.) He frequently speaks of life as a journey, as he does in the second sample given. There he uses compass imagery to speak of God's grace; elsewhere he uses similarly vivid contemporary images to speak of heaven. Perhaps in our own age we have been so influenced by demythologizing, or are so afraid of being misunderstood or taken too literally, that we may be hesitant apart from funerals to speak so specifically about God's everlasting love. The church is one of the few places people can expect that death will be placed in the appropriate perspective.

It was Donne's own personal suffering that led him to speak tenderly and lovingly, as he does here and elsewhere. We might follow his approach: He seeks words of hope and encouragement out of the depth of his own pain that will enable listeners to become what God would have them become. While we may only occasionally speak of our own experiences of suffering, we always preach out of suffering if we are to reach the hearts and souls of others in their pain. The range of Donne's metaphysical imagery—from earth to the heavens, from England across seas and continents, from horticulture to science and industry to theology, and from all manner of life experience—contributes to his communication of the depth of his own hope and the breadth of God's mercy.

Donne's principle of "inverting the text" can be essential for any preacher who wants to remain fresh and excited about preaching. If there was not sufficient hope in a passage, for instance in Martha's despair at Lazarus' death, Donne inverted the text to become a powerful profession of faith: "Lord, because thou wast here, our brother is not dead." Our standard test for this kind of hermeneutical exercise is in asking the question, Is this statement true of the faith as we understand it?

Inversion can also be used in an opposite direction to heighten hope. For example, Revelation 5:11-14 seems to be simply praise. Our problem is that we cannot move people to praise without first affirming where they may be (i.e., some distance from praise). Invert this text and we get a number of statements that are often true of our experience of the world: We do not hear angels and have no song in our hearts; we turn on the news and see only thousands and thousands of suffering faces; we wish there were a lamb on the throne, someone in control. Such honest identification of our experience in proclamation can lead then, in the latter part of the sermon, to a strong appropriation of the hope in the text.

CHAPTER 13

Alphonsus Liguori (1696–1787)
Redemptorist—the
Authority of the Terrible Moral

The spirit of reform that helped foster the Protestant Reformation continued within the Roman Catholic Church. For instance, in Italy an important reform group was the Oratory of Divine Love under the leadership of Catherine of Genoa and others in the early 1500s. The fruit of the Catholic Reformation included a renewal of the religious orders; the appearance of new societies, such as the Jesuits under Ignatius; a rebirth of mission work and renewed emphasis on preaching; clarification of doctrine and discipline by the Council of Trent (1545–1563); a formal ending of dialogue between Protestants and Roman Catholics by the same Council; and an overhaul of the administrative machinery of the church. Although the authority of Scripture became of increased importance, it was the authority of the organic church that remained central for Roman Catholicism.

Alphonsus Liguori was a key figure in the progress of the reforms in Italy. He was born of noble Neapolitan parents and trained and practiced as a lawyer until he lost an important case through an oversight, confusing one kind of law with another. Disillusioned with the justice system he united with a group of mission preachers, studied theology privately, and over the objections of his father was ordained in 1726. His power in preaching was soon recognized.

A nun had a vision and told him he was to help her group of nuns. He tested this revelation with his advisors and then helped reorganize the nuns in 1731. The next year he reorganized a group of priests. When he suggested that he would draw up a rule whereby they would live in poverty and utmost simplicity, most of the priests deserted him. He stood his ground, the numbers grew, and with papal approval they became known as the Congregation of the Most Holy Redeemer (Redemptorists) in 1749. They were a preaching order, dedicated to imitating Christ particularly through evangelizing the poor in the countrysides.

In 1762 he was appointed as a bishop and continued his reform work in the broader church. Controversies that dogged the Order throughout his lifetime were not settled before his death. He wrote approximately 100 books on subjects ranging from preaching to science, and was recognized as a systematizer of moral theology, intended to help both preachers and priests who were hearing confessions. His Order has since spread throughout the world.

Homiletical Setting

Because of the centrality of preaching for his Order, Alphonsus devised a fascinating and detailed homiletic, which is collected in one volume of his *Works*.[1] He covers all aspects of mission preaching, some of which we may list:

1) Missions would last for two or three weeks, led by two to twenty priests, and would be repeated every three or four years. They would follow the same pattern. There would be preaching for more than an hour in the morn-

ing and in the evening (Alphonsus would do the latter if he were present). His first sermon was on mortal sin and on the need for confession. For several days thereafter he would preach *di terrore,* that is, on the fear of the last things (death, judgment, hell). For several additional days he preached on the discipline of devout life. The remaining days would be occupied with the communion, in turn, of children, unmarried women, married women, and men. Meanwhile, during the days, priests heard confessions and taught catechetical classes to the separate groups. Priests could take no money, could ask for no food, but were allowed to ask for shelter.

2) In addition to the hour-long "great sermon," priests were to be skilled at four other kinds of exhortation. *Day and evening* exhortations were a form of 15- to 30-minute street-preaching to encourage people to come to the church to hear the sermon. These were usually based on the words of a preceding hymn and followed a set structure: introduction and proposition, amplification, moral application, announcement of the mission's purpose, and conclusion with a "terrible Sentence" warning of the judgment that approached. The exhortations to do *penance*— including the penance of "trailing the tongue on the ground" in contrition for blasphemy—was reserved for the men and followed the evening sermon. In the last days of the mission there were exhortations to *acts of peace and reconciliation.*

3) The structure of the "great sermon" followed a classical rhetoric rewritten by Alphonsus and inspired mainly by Quintilian and Paul. Invention dealt with having something to say, determining the intrinsic and extrinsic topics in a particular subject. Disposition dealt with the parts (*exordium*—general proposition, connection, particular proposition, division; *proof*—introduction, points and subpoints, refutation of objections; and *peroration*—epilogue [recapitulation], moral application, exhortation).

Elocution dealt with elegance of expression, harmony of composition, and dignity in figures of speech. To the classical canon, Memory, he devotes only a paragraph.

4) Near the end of the sermon the preacher might encourage the congregation to kneel and repeat words in an act of contrition. The preacher would also strike himself with a rope as an act of penance on behalf of the congregation. A blessing would be given with the crucifix.

5) Visual aids were used: the rope as a scourge in acts of contrition; a human skull (another common aid for spiritual contemplation) in the sermon on death; a large picture of someone who was damned was processed for the sermon on hell (the same picture would be blessed the next night).

6) The "bread of the divine word" was to be broken for the people in a manner so as to be sure they understood, as dictated by the Council of Trent. Latin quotations were to be kept to a minimum and were excluded entirely from the children's sermon, or "little sermon," which took place in a separate teaching location during the "great sermon." Ornateness of style, abstract ideas, and any seeking of applause were forbidden. Examples were to be taken from the saints and common life. Alphonsus once stopped one of his priests mid-sermon and required penance for failure to speak simply. Weeping, not idle laughter, was to be sought from the congregation.

7) Scripture was read for its moral lesson. The approach was frequently allegorical. Two Liguori sermons are based on Jonah. In the first, Jonah stands for our sin that must be thrown overboard to stop the tempest of God's scourge. In the second, Jonah's story is an allegory of God punishing us in this life to spare us in the next.[2] Once the "particular proposition" was determined from Scripture, the text was left behind, and any text, ancient authority, or saint might be cited. The divisions of his own argument were minimally emphasized.

8) As with Augustine, the sermon was to delight the con-

gregation. The purpose of delight was to encourage the practice of what was learned. Preachers were to aim their sermons at the uneducated and to provide them with practical specific instructions that they might follow.

9) Although the terrors and judgments of hell were to be proclaimed, the preacher was often to speak of the love of God in order that obedience might be out of faith rather than out of fear of punishment.

Sermon Sample

Alphonsus frequently spoke on hell and punishment and did so with great force. This excerpt from "On the Pains of Hell" is based on Matthew 13:30 (burning the weeds and saving the wheat). After discussion of the pains of narrow confines, fire, smoke, thirst, stench, shrieks, and lamentations, he concludes the sermon in the following way:

The reprobate, then, shall be tormented in all the senses of the body. They shall be also tormented in all the powers of the soul. Their memory shall be tormented by the remembrance of the years which they had received from God for the salvation of their souls, and which they spent in labouring for their own damnation; by the remembrance of so many graces and so many divine lights which they abused. Their understanding shall be tormented by the knowledge of the great happiness which they forfeited in losing their souls, Heaven, and God, and by a conviction that this loss is irreparable. Their will shall be tormented by seeing that whatsoever they ask or desire shall be refused. "The desire of the wicked shall perish"—*Ps.*, cxi. 10. They shall never have any of those things for which they wish, and must for ever suffer all that is repugnant to their will. They would wish to escape from these torments and to find peace; but in these torments they must for ever remain, and peace they shall never enjoy.

Perhaps they may sometimes receive a little comfort or at least enjoy occasional repose? No, says Cyprian. . . . The damned must remain for ever in a pit of fire, always in torture, always weeping, without ever enjoying a moment's repose. But perhaps there is some one to pity their sufferings? At the very time they are so much afflicted, the devils continually reproach them with the sins for which they are tormented, saying: Suffer, burn, live for ever in despair: you yourselves have been the cause of your destruction. And do not the saints, the divine mother, and God, who is called the Father of Mercies, take compassion on their miseries? No. . . . [The guilty have] voluntarily brought themselves to perdition.[3]

Implications

Alphonsus understood himself to be continuing the traditions of the early fathers, of classical rhetoric, and of scholastic theology. In the passage just quoted, his method mirrors his message. There is no escape from the consequences of sin, and he does not relent in his preaching even for a moment to allow comfort. The repeated sentence structure builds and maintains the pressure. When he thinks we have experienced this sufficiently, three times he asks a question that might offer some escape. But there is none. This is very effective speaking, whatever we may feel about the psychology employed in the question.

Alphonsus' missions were thoroughly organized in a sophisticated manner with instructions for all matters and occasions of public speaking. He faced the same kind of criticisms that meet evangelical revivals today, namely that they disrupt the community, and their effects are shortlived. He said his critics were wrong, and he insisted on simplicity of preaching and simplicity of advocated practice to ensure effectiveness: practices such as adoration of the sacrament (i.e., the bread and wine as the Body of Christ), frequent confession, daily prayers, and attendance at church. He understood that preaching leads to delight, delight leads to obedience, and obedience leads to faith. This idea of practice fostering belief is one we tend to overlook in our preaching. We might pay more attention to the requirements of faith within our own traditions by specifying beliefs and actions that follow from the sermon and that we hope will be followed by our people.

A similar point may be made concerning ethics and preaching. Although Alphonsus was a moral theologian and devised a method of moral discernment known as equiprobabilism (i.e., choose the milder of two equally probable or possible options), he avoided fine points in his preaching. In our own age we are often hesitant to speak as boldly as he does. It might be fruitful for us, corporately and individually, to identify topics and understandings about which we can speak with great confidence and certainty as we plan our preaching year. In a time of increased use of the lectionary and its subsequent influence in shaping our Christian education programs, we need to be careful that the individual needs of our congregations are not overlooked.

Already by Alphonsus' time there was a well-established practice, at least in Catholic missions, of having a "great sermon" for the adults and a "little sermon" for the children in a separate location. We may not have much better alternatives today. If we choose to make all our sermons intergenerational, we strip preaching of much of its potential. Yet if our children are in Sunday school during worship, they grow up with little practice of our worship traditions.

CHAPTER 14

Jonathan Edwards (1703–1758)
*Congregational—the
Authority of Experience, and
the Promised Land*

Jonathan Edwards was the foremost theologian to emerge in colonies of eighteenth-century America. He entered the recently chartered Yale College at age twelve and graduated from divinity studies at age seventeen. His father was a Congregational pastor, as was his grandfather on his mother's side, Solomon Stoddard, whom he first assisted and then succeeded in the important pulpit of the Congregational church in Northampton, Massachusetts, in 1729.

The Puritan settlers of New England were of various strands. Puritans espoused Calvinist theology and sought to "purify" the Church of England through reforms that went beyond those of Queen Elizabeth. They sought to remove any Roman influence and to restore to England true doctrine, pure worship, and correct discipline. In addition to moderate Puritans there were Presbyterians, who sought to replace the episcopacy with a presbyterial system, and Congregationalists, who sought independent "gathered" congregations, each with Christ as its head, and the overthrow of the episcopal order of the Church of England. Some were Separatists, who wanted to separate from, rather than reform, the state church.

In 1582 a law was passed that made treasonable any worship that did not conform with the Church of England. Many Non-conformists were imprisoned. With the succession of James I in 1603, and Charles I in 1625, Non-conformists were placed under increased pressure. Some Congregationalists fled, first to the Netherlands, and then 40 went to America on the *Mayflower* (most of the ship's 102 passengers were not Puritan), landing by mistake in Plymouth harbor on December 21, 1620, after three arduous months at sea. (They were aiming for the Puritan colony started the decade earlier in Virginia.) Although half of their number died that first winter, by 1640, with Archbishop Laud's intent to rid the church of Calvinists, there were 20,000 Puritans in Massachusetts. Many of these were highly educated and helped establish Harvard University in 1636. In England the remaining Puritans gained political favor between 1640 and 1660 (the time of the Long Parliament and Cromwell), suffered the Great Persecution after 1662, and gained religious freedom only with the Toleration Act in 1689.

The Puritans brought to America Calvinist hopes for building "God's kingdom here on earth," a commonwealth or ideal society under God's Word. The church valued education and trained the society, but did not itself seek to rule. An educated clergy which frequently proclaimed the Word was central to community self-understanding. Only church members could vote and only individuals who were born-again and could point to the experience of grace in their lives were allowed to be church members. By the second generation many were not having a born-again experience, and this requirement had to be modified. By Jonathan

Edwards' time attempts at uniformity had failed, the Salem witch hunts were over, and there was now some progress toward broad religious toleration. Understandings concerning the equality of "the elect" were extending beyond the church to lay the foundations for democracy. On the negative side, successive wars with Native Americans and internal church conflicts over issues like membership, discipline, communion, and structure were leading to widespread spiritual indifference.

Edwards decided to become a minister when, after Yale, he experienced what he called in a sermon, "a divine and supernatural light." It was a direct apprehension of God and a new sense of God's glory revealed in Scripture and in nature. His 1734 sermon series, "Justification by Faith Alone," resulted in a religious revival in Northampton, and his written account of the revival became famous at home and in Europe. His preaching, together with that of Methodist George Whitefield and the New Jersey Presbyterian, Gilbert Tennent, was largely responsible for the Great Awakening, a spiritual revival movement of 1740–1743. In 1749 he opposed his own church's open communion policy and was removed from office. He spent several years writing theology while ministering in a frontier mission church, and died of smallpox shortly after he became president of the College of New Jersey (now Princeton University). He and Sarah Pierpont had twelve children. His published sermons were widely read by succeeding generations.

Homiletical Setting

Several thrusts may be identified in Edwards' homiletic: 1) The Centrality of Personal Experience: John Locke argued that experience, not innate ideas, was the basis of thought. Edwards' homiletic is marked as much by Locke as it is by his own experience of conversion. He was against sober, intellectual religion and in favor of evangelical religion of the heart, founded in holy love. He preached that salvation was dependent upon a person's experience of God's glory. Preaching, the sacraments, and even terror could be used by the Holy Spirit as a converting ordinance.

2) The Maintenance of Community Order and Discipline: Puritan preachers were expected to assess the well-being of the community in their sermons, even as the pastor's family was to provide the model for the community life, not least in the practice of daily family devotions. During the Great Awakening, for instance, Edwards preached a series against those who were disrupting ecclesial and civil order with their violent inner experiences of God, yet who did not show outward signs of God's grace in their lives (*Treatise Concerning Religious Affections*).

3) America as a Threshold of Christ's Reign and World Salvation: Redemption is the central doctrine for Edwards. The revival in his Northampton, and generally in America, would help usher in the kingdom of Christ that would spread learning, peace, justice, and the end of persecution to the entire world. History was divided into three periods of redemption, each corresponding primarily to one person of the Trinity. The entire created realm was progressing irresistibly toward goodness and God's immanent self-glorification. These millenarian ideas are repeated themes in his work and were systematically expounded in a 1739 series of thirty sermons (all based on one verse, Isa. 51:8!—cf. *A History of the Work of Redemption*). These sermons represented an "entire new method" of combining scripture, theology, and history.

4) Images Functioning as Interpretative Symbols: His use of typology is similar to that of his predecessors except in two regards—(a) Christ is the redemptive reality presented not just in the Old Testament figures, types, images, and "shadows," but also in current events and nature; (b) Edwards devises an elaborate interpretative symbol system that is essentially his own. It is largely based on his understanding of Scripture and the book of Revelation as "visionary" and "metaphorical," not literal.[1]

5) Five Basic Models for Imagery of Redemption: He identified five central models (what literary critic Northrop Frye would call "archetypal images") of redemption that have scriptural warrant and may be found repeating themselves throughout time. All are actions: a turning "wheel of a chariot" (hence machinery and clocks); building "a great building" (hence plans and workers); a growing tree (hence growth and progress); a flowing river (hence commerce, trade, and progress); and "carrying on a war" (hence organization, sacrifice, and purpose).[2]

6) Typical Puritan "Plain Style" Sermons: Edwards' preaching is typical of the "plain style" the Puritans brought with them from England: **exposition** (if he is preaching a series of sermons on the same text, exposition is present only in the first one), followed by the statement and development of the **doctrine** (or theme) in its divisions, with reference to authors, history, common sense, and current events, and concluded with the **application** (or "improvement" or "use"). The application may vary in length from one third to two thirds of the total. The three-part style is simple and direct. The use of language displays a homespun informality and imagination, the sort that might derive in part from the Puritan use of narrative in their daily diaries to trace their "pilgrim's progress" as an individual.

Sermon Sample

The following famous words are from "Sinners in the Hands of an Angry God":

The God that holds you over the pit of hell, much as one holds a spider or some loathsome insect over the fire, abhors you, and is dreadfully provoked; his wrath towards you burns like fire; he looks upon you as worthy of nothing else, but to be cast into the fire; he is of purer eyes than to bear to have you in his sight; you are ten thousand times so abominable in his eyes, as the most hateful and venomous serpent is in ours. You have offended him infinitely more than ever a stubborn rebel did his prince; and yet it is nothing but his hand that holds you from falling into the fire every moment. 'Tis ascribed to nothing else, that you did not go to hell the last night.[3]

Here is an example of one of his five "models" of redemption, the image of a turning compass. This passage may be compared with Donne's sermonic use of the same image (quoted in chapter 12) as a way of highlighting their different styles:

And however small the propagation of the gospel among the heathen here in America has been hitherto, yet I think we may well look upon the discovery of so great a part of the world as America and bringing the gospel into it, is one thing by which divine providence is preparing the way for the future glorious times of the church when Satan's kingdom shall be overthrown not only throughout the Roman empire but throughout the whole inhabitable globe, on every side and in all its continents. When those times come, then doubtless the gospel which is already brought over into America shall have glorious success. . . . And in all probability God has so ordered it that the mariner's compass, which is an invention of latter times whereby men are enabled to sail over the widest oceans when before they durst not venture far from land, I say, we may look upon this as a preparation of providence for what God intends to bring to pass in the glorious times of the church, viz. the sending forth of the gospel wherever any of the children of men dwell how far soever off, and however separated by wide oceans from those parts of the world that are already Christianized.[4]

Implications

Many preachers today think of writing books but find it difficult to make time. Preachers of former ages, such as Edwards, used their sermon preparation as time also for book manuscript preparation. Sermons, however much revised, became books and treatises in a broader ministry beyond the parish. Whether this will continue to be possible with lectionary-based biblical preaching remains to be seen; it may be that the themes will be derived from the Christian seasons of the year, or that we still need to chart ways of returning to thematic preaching that will be responsible to the biblical texts.

Too often today an emphasis on personal experience in preaching is assumed to be removed from concerns either for social justice or for scholarly research. This is a recent development and does not characterize either the earliest or all modern expressions of evangelical faith as found in North America. Personal experience is still at the heart of any Christian profession of faith. Motivation to social action beyond the community depends upon preachers first speaking to individual experience in the community. Most people cannot respond wholeheartedly to the needs of others if their own needs and experiences have not first been named and affirmed, for it is out of personal encounters with God that we are opened to recognize the cohumanity of our neighbors, near and far.

It is curious to see that the separation of church and state in the United States has in some ways spawned a closer identification and occasional confusion of faith with national identity than has generally occurred elsewhere in the Western world. Although there have been benefits from civil religion, there have also been costs. Our religious forebears like Edwards gazed upon America as the Promised Land, one with the potential of saving the world. At the same time, they bore attitudes, for instance toward native peoples, that today we name racist.

Edwards' vision of Christ's imminent return was not predominantly doomsday judgment with God dangling us over the fires of hell. His optimism about the direction of history is an important reminder to preachers like us who live in less optimistic times. The gospel is Good News. This means that whatever else we preach, we preach hope, and when our own despair with the directions of the world becomes too great, we still preach hope and we continue preaching hope. The word *preaching* contains within it the word *reaching,* and often as preachers we are called to reach, through the Word we proclaim, to a truth we affirm that may be beyond our experience of the moment. Never do we give in to that which is the opposite of faith, no matter how tempting and powerfully persuasive it may be.

CHAPTER 15

John Wesley (1703–1791)
Methodist—the Authority of Law and Gospel

John Wesley is less remembered for his preaching than the fiery George Whitefield, who first introduced an initially hesitant Wesley to the experience of field-preaching. And yet if we thumb through Wesley's *Journal* we see large crowds gathering to hear him. On his first occasion of field-preaching on April 2, 1739, he preached to 3,000 persons—on a Monday! By June of that year he was preaching to nearly 14,000 at Blackheath.

This was a time of rapid urbanization and industrialization in England. The parish structures of the Church of England had not kept up with the economic and demographic changes. Huge sections of the population were unemployed or working in oppressive conditions and not being reached by the church. Outdoor preaching helped to alleviate the grayness of life and provided hope for those who were hungry for and therefore receptive to meaning. Wesley's preaching held crowds and helped to spread Methodist societies—one of many kinds of societies that existed in the church. Eventually his sermons became a cornerstone for the Methodist movement in another way: They were regularly published and used, in part, in the doctrinal training of Methodist lay and ordained preachers.

John Wesley was the eighteenth child of Samuel, a scholarly Anglican rector, and Susanna Wesley, whose education of her children was instrumental in shaping their lives. They were in the remnant Non-conformist Puritan strain of Anglican piety and discipline. John was saved at the last moment from fire in the thatched rectory at Epworth in 1709, and his mother taught him he was "a brand plucked out of the burning." Ordained in 1728, he joined his younger brother Charles, George Whitefield, and friends in an Oxford group called the "Holy Club" devoted to the pursuit of holiness through disciplined and methodical religious study (thus the initially pejorative label "methodists") and through social service, including visiting prisons and workhouses, teaching literacy, and distributing food.

Wesley fled back to London from a largely unsuccessful mission to Georgia (1735–1737) under legal threat. It was not until a meeting of Moravian Brethren, a German Pietist sect, on Aldersgate Street in London on May 24, 1738, that he became convinced of his own salvation through an experience of his heart being "strangely warmed" during the reading of Martin Luther's commentary on Romans. The truth he had preached became now the truth he had experienced. Thereafter he preached salvation by faith alone, a message that saw him regularly barred by local decision from preaching again in many of the Anglican pulpits he visited. He said that the "world is my parish." He particularly sought to awaken the faith of the masses and to have them turn to the church (as was currently happening in the German Pietist movement). To meet the demand he was persuaded, partly by his mother, to allow lay-people to preach: In 1710, while her husband was away for some months, she held Sunday night worship in her home as a way of nurturing the local people. At these meetings she had felt called by God to read the sermons, for "I do not think one man among [those present] could read a sermon without spelling a good part of it."[1]

He married on the rebound in 1751, and perhaps for that reason, along with work, he was rarely home. He traveled extensively in Great Britain and Ireland, preaching wherever and whenever he could, often one thousand times a year (often repeating material from his collection of sermons), except during the time of a scheduled local parish service. He set up Methodist societies, eventually in their own buildings, with rules for weekly "class meetings" of twelve members each divided by sex and marital status (thus many women were given leadership roles). These were devoted to mutual encouragement and nurture. He saw his movement as complementary to the sacramental functions of the church, to which he urged his followers' faithful attendance. Only in 1784, when he ordained as American presbyters two lay-preachers and sent the Reverend Dr. Thomas Coke to superintend and organize American Methodism with Francis Asbury, did he imply the independence of the societies from the Church of England. He denied being a separatist to his death in 1791.

Homiletical Setting

Wesley's Aldersgate experience convinced him that all that was necessary for salvation was a simple "saving faith" (i.e., justification) in Jesus Christ as Savior and Lord, through whom one was justified before God. Wesley believed, against Calvin, that saving grace is free for all, unrestricted and without limit, eliminating any possibility of predestination or prior principle of election. The goal of the Christian life was to seek not simply salvation but sanctification, a holiness that represents the "fullness of faith."

No ideas were more central to his preaching than his ideas of law and gospel. In 1779 Wesley gathered his ideas found throughout his writings in an article he published as an open letter.[2] It was an attack on those who would preach only law or only gospel. The Christian preacher must hold both in tension. Neither one could be abandoned. Law was "explaining and enforcing the commands of Christ comprised chiefly in the Sermon on the Mount." It slayed sinners in order that they might be raised by the gospel into spiritual life. For those who were already "pressing on to the mark" of sanctification and glorification, it was a "privilege" and "glorious liberty." Gospel, by contrast, was keeping "the love of Christ continually before [the congregation's] eyes, that thence they might draw fresh life, vigor and strength to run the way of his commandments." Each might be preached "in their turns," or "both at once," as was the case with all the "conditional promises" of the faith.

Wesley defends this method of preaching as "the scriptural way, the Methodist way, the true way." He says this in part because of the holiness journey. It goes from God's initial act of "preventing grace," to "convincing grace" or repentance, to justification by faith, to sanctification. It is essentially a journey from law to gospel. This process of salvation, he says elsewhere, is "both instantaneous and gradual."

Further points may be observed from his 132 sermons:[3]

1) His sermons are a version of the traditional "plain style" (exposition, doctrine, application). His introductions simply lay the groundwork for the sermon rather than begin his subsequent argument. The introductions may be as long as ten paragraphs (e.g., Sermon 21) or may be nonexistent (e.g., his thirteen-part series on the Sermon on the Mount). Most commonly they are two to four paragraphs long, and the last paragraph sketches the

sermon outline in two to four principal divisions with headings (e.g., "I shall endeavour to show first . . .; secondly . . .; and finally . . . .").

2) His sermons are published with a biblical text of usually one verse and rarely more than three. When there is exposition of a biblical text, it is within the introduction. He makes no attempt to treat a text verse by verse; he has no expository sermons. Once he is into the body of a sermon, his doctrine takes over. In the course of any sermon, biblical verses are quoted as they come to his mind. Sometimes he even returns to his stated text! (see Sermon 127). The last sectional division of his sermon is frequently reserved for some practical application.

3) It is unusual for him to consider an entire pericope or parable. One quarter of his published sermons are based on the Old Testament. Neither the biblical text nor the sermon deals with the liturgical season or church year, perhaps because he often preaches outside the church: There are no sermons specifically devoted to Advent, Christmas, Lent, or Easter.

4) One of Wesley's original rules for members of Methodist societies was that they "should attend the church and sacraments." Wesley does little in his published sermons to promote his rule.

5) From 1738 (post-Aldersgate) to 1746, most of his published sermons move from law (mixed with some gospel) to gospel (mixed with some law). For instance, "Christian Perfection" (Sermon 40) devotes its first half to the sense in which Christians are not perfect and its second half to the sense in which they are. But from 1746, when his sermons enter publication as instruction (and perhaps because they are instruction), there is no pattern, and law tends to dominate.

6) In his early mature years he perfected the peroration of classical rhetoric. He offers a stirring summary and emotional appeal as a conclusion. This too disappears after

1746 and returns only in the sermons of the 1780s, his last decade of life, along with a renewal of interest in rhetorical flair.

7) Accounts from witnesses indicate that he often used anecdotes, although there is no evidence of this in his manuscripts, and that occasionally he seemed unprepared.[4]

He and his Methodists became known for pioneering work in prison, legal, and workplace reform; civil rights; the abolition of slavery; and public education.

Sermon Sample

Here is an excellent example of Wesley's skill at the peroration, from his sermon "Justification by Faith" (1746):

Thou ungodly one who hearest or readest these words, thou vile, helpless, miserable sinner, I charge thee before God, the judge of all, go straight unto him with all thy ungodliness. Take heed thou destroy not thy own soul by pleading thy righteousness, more or less. Go as altogether ungodly, guilty, lost, destroyed, deserving and dropping into hell, and thou shalt then find favour in his sight, and know that he justifieth the ungodly. As such thou shalt be brought unto the "blood of sprinkling" as an undone, helpless, damned sinner. Thus "look unto Jesus"! There is "the Lamb of God, who taketh away *thy* sins"! Plead thou no works, no righteousness of thine own; no humility, contrition, sincerity! In no wise. That were, in very deed, to deny the Lord that bought thee. No. Plead thou singly the blood of the covenant, the ransom paid for thy proud, stubborn, sinful soul. Who art thou that now seest and feelest both thine inward and outward ungodliness? Thou art the man! I want thee for my Lord. I challenge *thee* for a child of God by faith. The Lord hath need of thee. Thou who feelest thou art just fit for hell art just fit to advance his glory: the glory of his free grace, justifying the ungodly and him that worketh not. O come quickly. Believe in the Lord Jesus; and *thou*, even *thou*, art reconciled to God.[5]

Implications

What gives some moments of preaching more power than others? Here there are several reasons we may cite: (1) This concluding paragraph is an effective summary of the message of his larger sermon, so Wesley does not have to concentrate on developing doctrines but can speak of them plainly; (2) he is speaking directly, as though personally, to each listener; (3) underlying the law of his forceful words is the powerful and simple gospel message that we can trust only in God and that God alone is trustworthy; (4) emphasis is on that which is eternal; and (5) he pays attention not merely to content but also to emotion and form. The sentences are short. The rhythm and pace is fast. The underlying message is that it matters what we do.

During Wesley's mid-career, with the arduous struggles of overseeing a vast, rapidly expanding movement, the Good News thrust turned up missing, at least from his published sermons. Too often our own temptation under the pressures and strains of modern ministry can be to ignore the proclamation of the Good News in favor of focus on our collective and individual duties and failures. This may instruct but will not long nourish those who are hungry for the goodness that God offers.

What made preachers like Wesley and Whitefield heard out of doors when they were preaching to thousands? They devised a way of projecting their voices that was close to singing. We know how a singing voice can carry farther than a spoken one. Even when we are using a microphone we should be speaking as though we do not have one: not shouting, or straining the voice, or speaking in an unnatural manner, but breathing from the diaphragm, allowing our stomach muscles to work in assisting our projection (even to the degree that they may even ache after we have spoken), such that the effect is a heightened naturalness. Proper breathing is to public speaking what location is to a retail business. We can be training ourselves every time we use our voice.

The tradition of heartfelt religion, of which Wesley is both a part and a founder of one branch, has tended to emphasize experience and emotion, and in preaching to call for passion. Henry H. Mitchell wisely calls passion "celebration."[6] This is the right note to sound if we are seeking to make our own preaching more passionate (however tempered we may seek to be). Often preachers mistakenly identify passion with anger. When they are wanting to sound passionate, they are only sounding angry. It is right to feel anger at and to preach against the sins of the world. It is inappropriate, however, to preach the anger that naturally arises in relation to individuals in our congregations and is best dealt with elsewhere. The Word of God is the issue, not how we might personally feel. Passion for preaching best arises out of a sense of the goodness of God's news for the world and both the urgency and immediacy of it. We are reaching, with all of the energy we possess, to make tangible that goodness, for ourselves and others, even as we preach it. Our words themselves communicate passion best when we avoid telling our congregation what to feel, and instead focus on creating the event that generates the feeling, thereby allowing individuals to experience it.

CHAPTER 16

Horace Bushnell (1802–1876)
Congregational—the Authority of Imagination

Two leading Protestant thinkers appeared in North America prior to the twentieth century. Both were preachers: Jonathan Edwards and Horace Bushnell. Although some of Bushnell's near contemporaries may be better known, arguably none is as significant: This includes preachers like revivalist and abolitionist Charles Finney (1792–1875); Henry Ward Beecher (1813–1887), son of Lyman Beecher for whom the Yale preaching lectures are named; Episcopalian bishop Phillips Brooks (1835–1893), whom Bushnell greatly influenced; Dwight L. Moody (1837–1899), who reached out to the urban unchurched masses; and Thomas DeWitt Talmage (1832–1902), who used the newspaper media to carry his messages.

Bushnell represents a turning point in Protestant thought as it moves from the rigidity of Calvinist doctrinal concern toward the emerging "new theology" of liberal American Protestantism. He was born in Connecticut and reared in the Congregational church, although his father was Methodist and his mother was a devout Episcopalian (she dedicated him to the ministry before he was born). After Yale he dabbled in journalism, law studies, and tutoring, but was eventually persuaded by a revival sweeping Yale to enter the ministry. In 1833, the year in which he married Mary Apthorp, he was called to North Church in Hartford where he ministered to a largely middle class congregation until poor health forced his retirement in 1859.

A collapse of health had also been the reason for spending 1845 in Europe where he wrote the first version of his famous work on educating Christians, *Christian Nurture* (1847; rev. 1861). His own young son had died just two years earlier, in 1843. Against Calvinist and Methodist tradition, he argued that children were best brought into the faith through gradual training in the family-like setting of a true Christian congregation rather than by experiences of fire and brimstone, sudden conversion, and revivals. This book was both comprehensive and radical for his time. In 1848 he experienced a "dawning of light" and new faith in the gospel that spoke to him of God's continuing act of creation in restoring us to our natural state. Two subsequent Trinitarian works, *God in Christ* and *Christ in Theology*, offended both Unitarians and those conservatives who sought to try him for heresy. Revealed truth and Christ's humanity were not given much attention in Bushnell's early works.

He was attempting to devise a method for mediating theological disputes and divisions based on consensus and experience. He reaped controversy instead. Eventually, in 1852, his congregation left the local Congregational association to distance itself from determined defenders of orthodoxy. Like many New England theologians, he tended to identify progress of Christian civilization with God's ability to bring good out of evil. He was active in the Second Great Awakening in New England in 1857–58 and continued writing and preaching during his fifteen years of retirement.

Homiletical Setting

If we had to isolate four broad ideas at the heart of Bushnell's theological method, it might be these. The first is the idea of *analogy:* There exists between our moral nature and God a "grand analogy, or almost identity."[1] This analogy is present in language itself, insofar as it is dependent upon physical objects, nature, and natural laws: Language contains an analogy of the intelligence of God imparted through symbols.[2] Doctrines are valuable only according to their ability to reveal God's nature and transform moral and spiritual life. For instance, the Lamb of Revelation 22:1 is useless if conceived separate from God. The Lamb must be conceived rather "with God internally." Bushnell wanted no Lamb whose nature was not relational to our sin and redemption, no Lamb who could not endure an enemy.[3] Dogma is essential but should be subservient to the inner supernatural light of knowledge given by the Spirit.

Bushnell argued that revelation was meant to be assessed with a view to its practical moral end. Atonement theories that argued "satisfaction" of an angry God were particularly in need of revision. Instead, Christ's atonement reflects God's love through the "double administration" of law and gospel. In life around us we find "analogies of law and gospel" (or what he also called "subatoning ways of discipline" and "analogical sub-gospels") in various levels of community life. In five "Great Analogies" of life (in some ways like Edwards' five models), we may find revealed God's intent for humanity, expressed in the movement from discipline to liberty: a parent teaching character to a child; a student learning to love knowledge; a laborer becoming skilled; army discipline enabling survival; and civil law allowing freedom.[4]

Two other ideas relate to the first. One of these is that

language is imprecise. Its function is to evoke awareness and truths that cannot literally be expressed. It is a human creation, a system of signs and symbols that has within it "an analogy of things," never to be confused with precise identity between a truth and its approximate representation in words, and never to be confused with science. In fact he denied to theology any possibility of exact rational science and thus to the Bible the possibility of strictly literal interpretation. "Human language," he says, "is a gift to the imagination so essentially metaphoric, warp and woof, that it has no exact blocks of meaning to build a science of."[5] The only way for communication of truth is to come at the subject from many sides: "Accordingly we never come so near to a truly well rounded view of any truth, as when it is offered paradoxically; that is under contradictions."[6]

The third idea is *the centrality of imagination* in the theological process. His essay, "Our Gospel, a Gift to the Imagination," gives his clearest articulation of this. All of the Bible—its histories, parables, epistles, even its prepositions!—is poetry and metaphor, signifying something beyond itself. Metaphor is not mere ornament but participates in the reality it addresses. Theology demands poetry, art, play, and the interpretative skills of a poet. Some in his day questioned the credibility of double meanings in Scripture. He argued there were many possible meanings, "even as a stalk of corn pushes out leaf from within leaf by a growth that is its unsheathing."[7] Meanings "double and redouble" depending on the typologies, images, or analogies we are devising.[8] His frustration with the Unitarians was their unwillingness to explore the symbolic potential of the Trinity, to which doctrine they gave instead only a literal reading. Knowing how difficult it was to reduce a poet's meaning to a few words, he found it amusing that Christians would try in doctrine to reduce "the grand poem of salvation" to "a few dull propositions." Imagination is essential if we are to understand symbol; to discover the core of Christ's message, who is himself "the metaphor of God; God's last metaphor!";[9] and to engage the people in the vitality of God's Word. Bushnell was a romanticist not least in believing Christians could be united in their "imagination forms" (i.e., metaphors) if they dropped their "word-logic forms" (i.e., rational attempts at literal discourse).

The fourth idea is that we should preach *Christ as the moral power of God in the world*. Bushnell develops this in an essay entitled "The Practical Uses and Ways of Preaching."[10] He was against preaching that reduced Christ to a great moral teacher; or the gospel to "an array of legal motives" and a matter of willpower; or the meaning of Christ's atonement to formulas about "penal suffering, expiatory death, literal substitution, judicial satisfaction, [or] legally imputed righteousness."[11] Rather Christ was to be preached as "moral power . . . the power of God unto salvation," the possibilities of which are endless and have to do with "all that He was, did, and expressed in His life and death and resurrection."[12]

Three things were necessary for Christ to be preached in power,[13] and each had to do with the recovery of what he understood as early Christian proclamation: (1) God's law and justice must be preached to "convince, intimidate, waken out of stupor [and] shake defiant wrong out of its confidences"; (2) the power is to be "personal," rooted in the "Gospel facts" of the personal witness to the incarnation, in the personal details of Christ's life and ministry ("dropping out all the accumulated rubbish of our wisdom"[14]—"I think it would be hardly possible for a preacher to be too much in the facts of His life"[15]); and (3) the power makes use of the "altar symbols" of sacrifice given to us by God as "our best means of grace," and most "objective." Through these worship symbols the metaphors of salvation become supernatural grace. The facts of Christ's life are laid out plainly in the preaching without "sacrifice," "simply a living and dying thus and thus." Christ is presented as "our sacrifice, an offering or oblation for us, our propitiation."[16] "He is my sacrifice . . . and beholding Him, with all my sin upon Him, I count Him my offering, I come unto my God by Him."[17]

Bushnell's own preaching deals immediately with the biblical text in one to several paragraphs, moves to his central idea or theme, and proceeds sometimes with points not usually identified in the introduction. Often he proceeds by way of finding truth within apparent contradictions or turns of phrase, by alternating between law and gospel, by probing fresh images, metaphors, and symbols, and by moving finally in the sermon hour to joyous proclamation. His sermon titles are often fascinating: "The Gospel of the Face" and "Free to Amusements, and too Free to Want Them."

Even as he was heavily influenced by Samuel Taylor Coleridge, his own work anticipates much current study in many fields, not least in language theory and metaphor (cf. McFague); myth, parables, and narrative (cf. Hans Frei); and doctrine (cf. Lindbeck).

Sermon Sample

In his Christmas sermon "Christ Waiting To Find Room," he first discusses the text in several paragraphs and then continues:

But I am anticipating my subject—viz., *the very impressive fact that Jesus could not find room in the world, and has never yet been able to find it.*

I do not understand, you will observe, that this particular subject is formally stated or asserted in my text. I only conceive that the birth of Jesus most aptly introduces the whole subsequent history of His life, and that both His birth and life as aptly represent the spiritual fortunes of His gospel as a great salvation for the world. And the reason why Jesus cannot find room for His gospel is closely analogous to that which He encountered in His birth—viz., that men's hearts are preoccupied. They do not care, in general, to put any indignity on Christ; they would prefer not to do it; but they are filled to the full with their own objects already. It is now as then, and then as now; the selfishness and self-accommodation, the coarseness, the want of right sensibility, the crowding, eager state of men, in a world too small for their ambition—all these preoccupy the inn of their affections, leaving only the stable, or some by-place, in their hearts, as little worthy of His occupancy and the glorious errand on which He comes.

See how it was with Him in His life. . . . [Bushnell now recites in turn numerous stories from Herod to Mary and Martha, the latter of whom did their best, but failed] fitly to receive the heavenful of honour and beauty brought into their house in His person. And so it may be truly said of Him, that He came unto His own, and His own received Him not. He was never accepted as a guest of the world, any more than on that first night in the inn. There was not room enough in the world's thought and feeling to hold Him or even to suffer so great a presence, and He was finally expelled.[18]

Implications

This is a passage typical of Bushnell at his poetic and doctrinal best. His use of language is outstanding. We might try some of his devices. Here we see his brilliant turns of phrase; his use of contradiction (i.e., we wish no indignity on Christ yet we lock him out); the recurring phrases that play on the idea of no room (i.e., "hearts pre-occupied," "filled to the full," "self-accommodation," "a world too small," "preoccupy the inn of their affections"); the clever scriptural echoes, analogies, or types that he finds; and the organic unity he builds into his prose through both image and idea. It is also interesting in his opening remark that he, and presumably his people, care about what actually is in the biblical text as opposed to what may be read into it.

There are many insights we may gain from Bush-nell. One is his concern for the practical end of doctrines. This can be an excellent test for our sermons that we can employ in part by asking ourselves, "What does it look like?" and "Does it preach?" We preach best when we know needs best. At issue is more than this. Bushnell brings fresh thought to doctrinal questions, and the vitality of his thinking contributes to its relevance. Doctrine in preaching need not be and should not be a matter of reciting by rote. If we do as he did, and recognize that most of our central doctrines of the faith are best expressed in part through paradox or contradiction (e.g., Christ died and is alive, in our death we find life, and so on), we can emphasize the two sides of the contradiction to make our preaching more vital. The truth that emerges is the truth discerned by faith.

His idea of "analogies of law and gospel" or "sub-gospels" is both intriguing and helpful. It identifies what we are looking for when we seek stories from experience around us and in world events: We seek analogies of salvation. Because of our own capacity for sin we can rarely speak with absolute assurance about how God is acting in particular situations. Jesus cautions against saying, "Lo here," or, "Lo there." But without always ascribing absolute identity, we can find analogies of God's action in a manner similar to the way Jesus spoke of the realm of God in his parables. At the same time, we never leave our preaching merely at analogy but go on to speak directly and forcefully of God in Christ and the Holy Spirit, as Bushnell was so skillful in doing.

Bushnell's use of imagination can be instructive to us. There is an unfortunate tendency today to identify imagination with a particular form of preaching (i.e., narrative). Bushnell understood imagination to be more than a mere synonym for creativity and an antonym for doctrinal reflection. Previous philosophy had implied that reason was the only means of apprehending knowledge, and that reason was served by the various senses and the intuitive ability of imagination to perceive likeness and difference. Bushnell, following Coleridge and Kant, argued that imagination was in itself a mode of both perception and discernment that complemented the different thought processes involved in the logic of reason. Understood as such, imagination is larger and more important for the theological enterprise than a mere equation with creativity (reason is also creative) and limitation to a particular form.

We may follow Bushnell's lead. He did not use imagination to adopt one particular sermonic form or to avoid explicit doctrinal reflection. Imagination was not the opposite of doctrinal reflection, it was the opposite of abstract doctrinal formulation that was disconnected from experience. He used imagination in three ways: (1) to put poetic language at the service of theology, (2) to recover the details of Jesus' life and ministry for preaching, and (3) to ensure that doctrinal reflection was directly related to the moral and spiritual needs of the church.

CHAPTER 17

Catherine Mumford Booth (1829–1890)
Salvation Army—the
Authority of "Aggression"

Catherine Mumford Booth and her husband William Booth (1829–1912), both reared in the Methodist tradition, co-founded The Salvation Army in London. She is only one of many women in Great Britain and America who had become preachers.[1] George Fox (1624–1691), founder of the Quakers, had approved of women preaching, as had Wesley (Sarah Mallet in 1787). It was nonetheless still unusual for women to speak in public, despite public pioneers like Quaker prison-reformer Elizabeth Fry (1780–1845). At this time women had no vote and few formal opportunities for education. Booth is one of the earliest of recent women from whom we have a large collection of sermons. While William excelled as an itinerant evangelist and organizer, she excelled intellectually and as a writer, orator, and fundraiser. She started regular services in London's trendy West End, where eventually she preached to many of the social elite and raised money for the Mission, located in the poverty of the working-class East End.

Educated at home by her mother, she became a devout social activist and fought for women's equality. At age twenty-one, she wrote to inquire of her local pastor, "Whether you have ever made the subject of woman's equality as a being, the matter of calm investigation and thought?" Two years later she wrote to her future husband, "Never till she [woman] is valued and educated as man's equal will [marital] unions be perfect and their consequence blissful."[2]

In 1859, visiting American evangelist Phoebe Palmer was attacked in a pamphlet for preaching. In response, Catherine, now the mother of three, published her famous ten-thousand-word pamphlet, "Female Ministry," defending Palmer and women's right to minister. (Palmer later donated her home in New York to become the first Salvation Army hospital in America.) Catherine herself began to preach after its publication only with much encouragement. She began publishing her sermons in book form only in the 1880s in part as a way of defending the Army from persecution: In 1884 alone, six hundred Army preachers were imprisoned and many more Army members were assaulted. In the same decade she was an active leader in a successful campaign to amend the criminal code to protect young girls from men and to end the white-slave trade.

The Christian Mission was founded by the Booths in 1865 as an evangelical movement balancing preaching and social welfare. In 1878, William, on the spur of the moment, wrote down "The Salvation Army" instead of "the volunteer army," and the name stuck. Uniforms, officers, volunteers, brass bands popular with the working class, corps (congregations), a newspaper called *The War Cry*, and even the flag Catherine introduced, all contributed to the divine battle against sin and suffering that was being waged.

Their initial intent, like that of Methodism as a whole, was to be a complement to existing churches, but their doctrines and "aggressive" conversion methods were misunderstood. Catherine published *The Salvation Army in Relation to the Church and State*, to spell out their social action, to affirm their belief in "the great fundamental doctrines of Christianity," and to indicate Army distinctiveness.[3] By then the Army had 528 corps or congregations in England, 245 field outposts, and 103 corps abroad. Following her recommendation, the Army had ceased celebrating the sacraments and cut anything deemed not essential to salvation. She published six books of sermons and lectures. Three of their children helped expand the movement worldwide, including Evangeline, who became a well-known preacher and national commander first for Canada and then the United States.

Homiletical Setting

Numerous features of Booth's homiletic, in addition to her advocacy for women and women's rights, may be identified:

1) Chief among these is what she called "our *aggressiveness*": "The Gospel idea of preaching is not merely laying the truth before men . . . but that a teacher . . . be possessed of sufficient Divine influence to thrust his message in upon the heart, to make the soul realize and feel his message."[4] She preached the need for an "antagonistic force of good," because churches were being outpaced by the population: "Just think that the Church, instead of *aggressing on this territory of the enemy,* is allowing that enemy to *aggress upon her!*"[5] She defended their methods: "Does it signify by what novel and extraordinary methods we get hold of the drunkards, wife-beaters, cutthroats, burglars, and murderers, so that we do get them?"[6] She said in the book entitled *Papers on Aggressive Christianity* that "real Christianity is, in its very nature and essence, aggressive," by which she meant witnessing to Christ without fear of giving offense.[7]

2) The only New Testament law for this aggressive warfare in preaching is "adaptation" or expediency. We "adapt ourselves and our measures to the social and spiritual condition of those whom we seek to benefit."[8] This meant capturing their interest, speaking at their level, and trying as many different approaches as possible.

3) She did not preach what she called "the 'only believe gospel.'"[9] She preached repentance, repentance that was more than conviction of sin, sorrow for it, or mere promising to do better. This was the "spurious repentance" of most churches. Real or true repentance was the renouncing of sin, was being saved and born again, was faith in Christ, obedience to God and to the power of God to transform personal life. It included renouncing dancing, alcohol, tobacco, jewelry and fancy clothes, personal wealth, and all self-centered behavior.[10]

4) Her sermons are pragmatic, focusing on conversion and moral behavior, not doctrine. They are logically and simply organized, often with points that are easily remembered (e.g., who, when, how).

5) She generally took her texts at their face value or obvious meaning. There was no arguing about fine points, which might be of little interest to her hearers. She might briefly treat a parable typologically (e.g., the Prodigal Son prefigures Jewish-Gentile relations) but then read it as an extended allegory about repentance.[11] Her basic principle of interpretation had ancient roots: "Take that which is plain and unmistakable as a key to unlock and interpret that which at first sight is difficult and contradictory."[12] She argued specifically against literalists, at least in her interpretation of the New Testament in "Female Ministry."

6) She frequently cited the needs of children and told moralistic stories of both men and women whom she encountered in her everyday life (sometimes with the purpose of instilling fear in those not saved). Her com-

ment in her lecture "The Training of Children" is typical of her sensitivity to women's issues: "I have sometimes thought, while I have heard men talking to women on their difficulties as wives and mothers, their trials and difficulties, and so on—'Ah, this is all very good, but you don't know much about it, after all.' Now, I do not come . . . under this disadvantage."[13]

Sermon Sample

Booth encourages her congregation to minister close to home:

Get your heart full of the living water and then open the gates and let it flow out. Look them in the face and take hold of them lovingly by the hand and say, "My friend, you are dying, you are going to everlasting death. If nobody has ever told you till now—I have come to tell you. My friend, you have a precious soul. Is it saved?" They can understand that! not beginning in a roundabout way, but talking to them straight. . . . Your rich neighbours and your servant-girls and your stable-men alike, can understand that.[14]

She speaks to her wealthy listeners on the subject of money in the same forthright manner that Chrysostom, for instance, had used to challenge his listeners to change their life-styles:

I once heard an old veteran saint say, and I thought it was extravagant at the time, "I consider the use of money the surest test of a man's character." I thought, no, surely his use of his wife and children is a surer test than that; but I have lived to believe his sentiment. . . . God never uses anybody largely until they have given up their money. I simply state a fact. We know it so by experience and the history of God's people. You must give up your money as an end: saving it for its own sake, or the gratification of your selfish purposes or those of your children—it must be all given to God, to whom it belongs, being entirely used in His service. If you want to be a successful laborer for souls, you will have to do that at the threshold. Give up your money to the Lord. If you think it right to keep some of it, keep it to use it for Him as you go; and be as strict with yourself, to your Heavenly Father, as you would be with your secretary or clerk to yourself, and then you will be all right.[15]

Implications

It took remarkable courage and confidence to do what Catherine Booth did in taking on the religious and social culture of the times, not least because she was a woman. She placed herself in situations on the street and at public meetings that invited ridicule and sometimes physical danger (she used a converted boxer as a bouncer and bodyguard). Her confidence stemmed from her faith, from the needs she saw in the poverty around her, and from her conviction that she was right. Many in all ages have been afraid to identify what they believe for fear of losing popularity. Few people who have achieved great things have avoided controversy. It is doubtful that Booth would have accomplished what she did if she had been compromising in her presentation of her faith. She assumed a tough parental role to those who may have lacked adequate parenting. We might ask ourselves, "In what situations in ministry today is it appropriate or inappropriate to adopt such a role?"

Another question we may ask is, How are we going to speak about money in our churches? Booth here is more radical than many in history who have spoken about the giving of tithes (a tenth portion of all) and offerings (any givings beyond the tithe). She does not say it, but she implies correctly that generous giving to the church is not just a duty, it is a spiritual discipline that opens us to receiving blessings that God wishes us to receive.

Throughout history people have used their own perceptions of truth to be the measure and judge of others. This happened to the Booths, and to some degree it was perpetuated by them as well. Our greatest strengths can also be our greatest weaknesses, and this could apply to the radicalism of "aggression." Often what we do in the name of truth or in the name of love can be the opposite of both. In preaching as in the living of our lives, when we feel most self-righteous, we are in danger of sinning.

Booth takes pride in what women's experience has to teach us. It is unfortunate how many preachers through history and even today manage to exclude women's experience from their preaching. Booth takes us right into people's homes, at times, and we meet the children by name and hear what the parents are actually saying. When we include similar contemporary experience in our preaching, of people near and far in all circumstances of life, it becomes more difficult for our sermons to become too abstract.

Booth criticized the way men speak of women's experience in preaching. A woman graduate student recently made a similar remark specifically about preaching on one aspect of women's experience. She noted that when some men preach about violence done to women and children, a very difficult area for men, they tend to recount the details and to encourage sympathy. What would be more helpful is for men to leave out the details, to identify how accounts of male violence make them feel as males, and to analyze how male ways of relating may contribute to violence.[16]

CHAPTER 18

Harry Emerson Fosdick (1878–1969)
*Baptist—the Authority of
Pastoral Counseling*

Harry Emerson Fosdick, a Baptist from upstate New York, played a formative role in shaping North American preaching for several reasons: his various ministries including his tenure as founding minister of Riverside Church in New York City (1930–1946); his weekly half-hour "National Vespers" NBC radio broadcasts to three million listeners; his large collection of published works, most of them anthologies of sermons; his contact with seminary students through his teaching (including homiletics) at Union Seminary (1908–1934); and, basic to all of these, his skill as a preacher and his modeling of a new alternative method of preaching.

Fosdick's ancestors were Non-conformist Puritans from Suffolk and Cheshire, England, who fled during Archbishop Laud's persecutions of the 1630s. Fosdick had a fiesty heritage. His grandfather in Buffalo, who was the first in his family to become a Baptist, was part of the underground railroad and helped to row escaped slaves across the Niagara River to Canada and freedom. He also fought for tax-supported public schools. His grandmother's father was a Baptist minister excommunicated for not believing in hell. His other grandmother was an ardent feminist, inspired by an 1848 Syracuse conference led by Elizabeth Cady Stanton and Lucretia Mott. The first independent decision Fosdick remembered making was his decision to be baptized at age seven, in spite of his parents' reservations about his youth.

The intellectual roots of the Baptist movement go back to the Anabaptists, radical Protestants advocating believer (not infant) baptism by immersion, congregationalist structure, and rejection of earthly authority. Their influence spread to English Puritans where there were Particular Baptists (Calvinists) and General Baptists (followers of Jacobus Arminius, i.e., Arminians, who said the atonement was not just for an elect few). Many came to follow Wesley's Holiness movement. In America, the Central Convention of Baptists (1814), strongly committed to missions and education, split over slavery and by Fosdick's time the separation of Northern and Southern Baptists was complete (1907). His ministry at Riverside was interdenominational.

Two experiences profoundly shaped his ministry. First, at Colgate University he rejected the inerrancy of the Bible and was rescued for ministry, he said, by the new liberal theology (which had been in the wind in Bushnell's time but had now formed hard lines between liberals and fundamentalists). It was based on reason and experience (i.e., of the Trinity) not metaphysical theories, and on historical-critical interpretation of the Bible. Second, as a student at Union Seminary and working also in New York's slums, he suffered a "nervous breakdown," which forced him to face his own human limitations. He began to rely on prayer and to consider preaching, not religious teaching, as his calling. His intense suffering led him eventually to place pastoral counseling at the heart of his preaching.

Fosdick was the first minister to support Alcoholics Anonymous publicly, and was known for his beautiful prayers, for his "modernist" belief in progress (largely influenced by the "Social Gospel" of Walter Rauschenbusch, 1861–1918), for his optimism about human nature (in contrast to the neoorthodoxy of his Union colleague Reinhold Niebuhr, or of Karl Barth), for his opposition to war (his 1934 sermon, designed as a confession to "The Unknown Soldier," helped place him at the head of the Protestant peace crusade and, inadvertently, of those favoring American isolationism), and for his advocacy of women's rights, civil liberty, and racial justice. Rarely are his sermons devoted to social issues, however. He was married to Florence Whitney, with whom he had three children.

Homiletical Setting

In journal articles in the 1920s, 1930s, 1950s, and in his autobiography, Fosdick discussed his "project method" of homiletics. It was in contrast to topical preaching, which he felt was a "Sir Oracle" lecture on a theme, and expository preaching, in which preachers "assumed that folk come to church desperately anxious to discover what happened to the Jebusites."[1] He outlined the contemporary expository preaching of which he was critical: "First, elucidation of a Scriptural text, its historical occasion, its logical meaning in the context, its setting in the theology and ethic of the ancient writer; second, application to the auditors of the truth involved; third, exhortation to decide about the truth and act on it."[2]

After floundering for his first years as a preacher, he devised a homiletic based in *pastoral counseling* that made preaching an adventure for him. Every sermon was to start with the "real problems of people"[3] and was to "meet their difficulties, answer their questions, confirm their noblest faiths and interpret their experiences in sympathetic, wise and understanding co-operation."[4] He looked for the way even large issues of the day, national and international, affected the lives of ordinary people. He wanted sermons to be conversational, "a co-operative dialogue in which the congregation's objections, questions, doubts and confirmations are fairly stated and dealt with."[5] The preacher's business is "to persuade people to repent . . . to produce Christian faith [and] to send people out from their worship on Sunday with victory in their possession." To this end, "A preacher's task is to create in his congregation the thing he is talking about."[6] A sermon on joy is to explore wrong ideas about it, false attempts at it, problems in getting it, and then move to create it.

Whereas lectures had "a *subject* to be elucidated," preaching had an "*object* to be achieved."[7] Determining this "object" or problem to be solved was the first step in preparation. This was followed by "free association of ideas," perhaps for several hours, followed in turn by exploration of literature, cases from counseling, the Bible, and personal experience. His structure, commonly three points, for which one must listen carefully to discern, often emerged in the writing of his sermons. Someone said his "sermons begin by describing a human need, next illustrate that need from literature, from contemporary events and personal experiences, and then turn to the Bible for those principles which could meet that need."[8] His critics caricatured his preaching as "undogmatic Christianity" and "problem-solving."

We may name some features that contribute to the distinctive Fosdick style:

1) His dialogue axis is "we" (i.e., his listeners) against "the powers of this world" (i.e., war, science, profit), not "we" against "them" (some group). He tends to exclude no one.
2) His casual familiarity with many subjects (history, philosophy, psychology, science—no subject was too specialized) and his grand, if somewhat sweeping generaliza-

tions about these topics, help him to create the impression that modern life is now brought into focus.

3) To his challenging questions he provides hopeful answers, which center on matters of personal faith and what we can do. For example, in his sermon "The Mystery of Life," he speaks first of the depth of mystery, even in the face of science, discusses our response, which is frequently to hide, and devotes the rest of the sermon to what is in the unknown and our appropriate attitude toward it.

4) His sermons move from problem to solution, from quandary to hope (Fosdick's own version of law vs. gospel), and from primarily intellectual appeal to primarily emotional.

5) Much of his intrigue lies in his ability to juxtapose opposing or contradictory images, ideas, or opinions, to speak to both sides of issues, and to move, in the process, to some form of resolution of the problem from a Christian perspective.

6) When the biblical text is the source of his "object" (perhaps a third of the time), the text generally appears near the beginning and at the end of the sermon. He normally looks for the personal experience implied in the biblical text.

Sermon Sample

In II Corinthians 12, Fosdick finds a distressed Paul recalling his earlier vision of a man "caught up into Paradise." It provides an excellent example of Fosdick finding his "object" or "project" in a biblical text:

Then into the midst of his [Paul's] discouraging present he interjects a factor that makes all the difference in the world to him. His high hours and what they have taught him, come back to him. Fourteen years before, he recalls one of them when vision cleared and the eternal verities were surely seen. Like a sailor on a foggy day having a tough time, he remembers his clear days when far horizons could be seen. And as one reads this worried letter, written out of a disheartening present, one sees this thing at least that is saving the man and making him rememberable yet across the centuries: he is believing the testimony of his best hours against the testimony of his worst hours as to what life really means.

Is not that one of the central problems of human life? Which are we to believe, our best hours or our worst? We have them both. . . . Surely, we need Paul's secret now. Many of us here are in a low mood, in a depressing year. We have won a war, but what a mess! It is foggy weather on a rough sea for all of us who care about the world, and I, for one, need to remember the clear days when I could see better.[9]

He goes on to say, (1) life's better hours are those when life is in relationship to God, (2) we are Christian when we trust our enlightened hours not our dark, and (3) out of crisis can come great hours.

Another sermon begins this way:

Recently the newspapers carried the story of a man who boarded a bus with the full intention and desire of going to Detroit, but when at the end of a long trip he alighted at the destination, he found himself, not in Detroit, but in Kansas City. He had caught the wrong bus. Something like that goes on habitually in human life. People on the whole desire good things [and] find themselves somewhere else altogether! . . . The Prodigal Son did not start out for a swine pasture.[10]

Implications

Fosdick was a preacher's preacher and a popular one: He had a creative use of language and imaginative thought, was easy to quote, and had a strong, positive message. It is hard to know whether the self-confident generalizations he made to summarize history and his time can still be made with effect today, in an era of acknowledged specialization. Perhaps we have to be more cautious to be plausible. But perhaps we are too cautious, hesitant to talk about any number of things which affect us in complicated ways. The issue is one of preacher's license: Does the art of persuasion not call for give-and-take between hard fact and moderate exaggeration for the purpose of effect?

Fosdick was sometimes rightly criticized for taking his message to the biblical text and for using the text to illustrate his predetermined point. When he does allow the text to speak on its own, as in the excerpts quoted, his reading has inherent interest, primarily because he is looking for the human experience within it. He refuses, as we ought to refuse as well, to allow biblical texts to be dry documents of a foregone age. In each of the passages quoted we also see how he sets up the opposites in his sermons to play against each other and to produce a dominant "spark" of imagination: the best hours versus the worst hours; the right bus versus the wrong bus. Out of that polarity emerges the "controlling image" or predominant metaphor of the sermon.

We can learn much from Fosdick's easy use of story, his assumed familiarity with his listeners, and his willingness to enter into the struggles of their personal lives. He is a pioneer trying to integrate preaching with the new discipline of psychology. North America was showing its fascination with individual psychological motivation. One of the best lessons he can teach us is, at some time in our preparation, to think through to the "object" of our preaching, to identify some need that our message meets, and to underline that in our preaching.

Another excellent lesson comes from his dialogue axis

between "we" and "the world." Whenever we preach we should do what Fosdick accomplished: Assume the best of even the worst person we might mention in a sermon, whether that person is in the biblical text, or from former times, or a contemporary of our own. The preacher might help us to understand the kind of experiences that might lead someone today to do an evil act. In exercising that ministry of generous love and compassion in our sermons, we are reaching out to those who may identify themselves in another's behavior.

Whenever we name a difficult issue for all of us, we may go one extra step. In addition to naming the issue, we might also probe farther to help us understand, from a theological perspective, what prevents us from changing our behavior. The issue might be our participation in the excessive materialism of our culture. To probe it we might consider whether we lack a sense of identity separate from the goods we buy. Or do we fear not being seen as a success? Or is it that in an impersonal world it is hard to feel connected to our underprivileged brothers and sisters? Whichever of these avenues we explore, we would then seek to provide a theological counterpoint (e.g., it is in Christ we find our true identity; or, in the eyes of Christ, our love alone is sufficient for success; or, it is our brothers and sisters, particularly those who are suffering, in whom we can expect to encounter Christ).

CHAPTER 19

James S. Stewart (1896–1990)
Presbyterian—the
Authority of Evangelical Tradition

The Presbyterian Church in Scotland was founded by John Knox (who left only three sermons). His church has produced many great preachers, and James S. Stewart, along with Thomas Chalmers (1780–1847), is one of them. Stewart belonged to the branch of Presbyterianism known as the Free Church, of which Chalmers was the first moderator after the Disruption of 1843. In contrast to its parent established church, the Church of Scotland (with which it reunited in 1929), the Free Church was opposed to any state interference in church affairs. It was born in the early 1800s out of the Protestant evangelical revival that followed Jonathan Edwards and John Wesley.

Stewart was born in Dundee, Scotland. His father was the son of a Y.M.C.A. secretary who had been converted to Christianity in a crusade by American evangelist Dwight L. Moody in 1872–74. During student days James made two ventures to continental Europe. One was with the Royal Engineers in France during World War I. The other, after his divinity studies at St. Andrews University, was at the University of Bonn on a year's scholarship. He served parishes between 1923 and 1947, primarily at North Morningside Church, Edinburgh. In addition to being joint editor of the English translation of Schleiermacher's *The Christian Faith*, he wrote articles and several books including a Bible study course for youth; a study of *Paul as a Man in Christ* (1935); three sermon anthologies; and *Heralds of God* (1946), his Warrack lectures on homiletics. A supplementary volume on the subject of evangelism was written for the Lyman Beecher Lectures and appeared as *A Faith to Proclaim* in 1953.

New College, Edinburgh, named him professor of New Testament in 1946, a position held until his retirement in 1966. Former students say that he was gracious, humble, private, quiet, and almost painfully shy, finding small talk both difficult and embarrassing. To avoid it, at student gatherings in his home he normally asked students for a topic to discuss. Yet when he entered the pulpit or the lecture hall, he was a passionate speaker. He was a traditionalist who avoided controversy and seemed little influenced by the neoorthodoxy of Karl Barth.

Stewart was less worried about threats to the church from "the secularism without" than he was about those from "the reduced Christianity within."[1] On one hand he heard those in a disheartened, war-torn Britain who argued that preaching was no longer relevant and should be less central in worship. On the other hand he heard preachers who (1) had turned to topical or thematic preaching in a search for relevance, or, (2) had turned away from doctrine because they found it dull—Freud seemed to have explained evil; sin and forgiveness were incompatible with an optimistic belief in progress—or, (3) had been so influenced by Bultmann and others that they had lost sight of the cross and resurrection in their preaching.

He was married to Rosamund Brown and had two sons. Like John Donne, he served as a royal chaplain, for thirty-nine years. He served in 1963 as moderator of his church, and held lectureships at Union Seminary (New York), Princeton, and Berkeley.

Homiletical Setting

Stewart, like Fosdick across the Atlantic, was a preacher's preacher. His strength was not innovation but evangelical tradition. There was one congregational test for preaching, "Did they, or did they not, meet God today?"[2] He believed that only sermons that *exalt Christ* are Christian sermons.[3] This is for him the one theme of preaching. Preaching Christ is a fourfold matter: It is preaching his death; his resurrection; the Realm of God breaking in with power; and God's action intervening in human history, not just in personal lives.[4] The cross should be preached so that it meets the world in a three-fold manner: as revelation of human sin; as the comfort of victory over sin ("After Calvary it can never be midnight again");[5] and as a challenge to listeners.[6]

He cautioned experimental preachers who would substitute cleverness for dogma that their ministry would wear out with no spiritual harvest: "I am insisting on what is paradoxical but true—that the more resolutely and stubbornly you refuse to be deflected from the one decisive theme, the greater the variety you will achieve."[7] Preaching should be *expository*, opening up the text. One should "let the Bible speak its own message,"[8] and avoid bringing alien meanings that are not the intent of the author. There could be "excessive literalist" interpretations even as there might be appropriate use of allegory in a "spiritual" line of interpretation.[9] Preaching should follow the Christian year and its own great doctrines. And the sermon should be well prepared and never borrowed even in part. Weekday mornings should be devoted to study, with the Sunday morning sermon completed by Wednesday night, and the evening one by Friday night.[10]

His method was to choose a text that had struck him in his devotional reading of the Bible and on which he had made notes in his notebook.[11] He would start by identifying an aim, intent, or central truth in a single sentence. Next he would do an exercise like Fosdick's: He would write, regardless of logical order, "all the thoughts, suggestions, illustrations which your chosen theme brings clustering into your mind." The written sermon might start either with the Bible or contemporary life (his most common mode) or, more ideally, with a combination of both. It is "bad psychology" to reveal one's divisions at the beginning of a sermon. The number of points should vary from sermon to sermon. He advocated both a decisive ending and cultivating "the quiet close": "You will never weaken the force of your final appeal by keeping it restrained."[12]

There are three collections of Stewart's sermons: *The Gates of New Life* (1940), *The Strong Name* (1941), and *The Wind of the Spirit* (1968). In these, several features become clear. His texts are usually only one or two verses, but he regularly opens entire stories or pericopes and retells them, freely adding narrative details to make them come alive. There is a majesty in his use of the English language and literature. Most of his illustrations are from Christian biographies or well-known poetry, novels, and drama. His sermons are affirming, point to mystery, and usually call for a commitment to Christ. They are hopeful, moving back and forth between what he called life on the wrong side of Easter Day and life on the right side, where his sermons always end. He stresses God as an actor in history and events. His *cross-centered preaching* contributes to his love of opposites and paradoxes (e.g., *Name*, pp. 116ff.; *Heralds*, pp. 13ff., 156). He uses romantic ideas (e.g., Jesus' "heroism") and generalizations (e.g., Christians are happier than others; "the New Testament [is] the most joyous book in the world"). It is rarely clear exactly how his New Testament scholarship contributes to his sermons—he does not discuss critical issues like redaction or form. He does not enter his own sermons or draw back the curtain on any of his personal life. Nor does he enter into social analysis or specific criticism of his time and culture.

Sermon Sample

Here is Stewart at his descriptive best, retelling the story of John 3:8:

Now here was Jesus with Nicodemus on the Mount of Olives. It was night, with the moon riding high above Jerusalem, and driven clouds scudding across the face of the moon. The wind blowing up from the valley was stirring the branches and rustling the leaves of the olive trees. Jesus was speaking to Nicodemus about the work of God in the soul and the new birth—how God could take a life that was conscious of failure and emptiness and dissatisfaction and sin, and transform it and make it full and strong and vital and victorious. But Nicodemus was not understanding. . . . [So Jesus said,] "Listen to the wind, Nicodemus! Listen to the wind! You can hear its sound—the night is full of it, hark to it in the tops of the trees—but where it has come from and where it is going no man knows. Now, Nicodemus, the Spirit of God is just like that—invisible yet unmistakable, impalpable yet full of power, able to do wonderful things for you if only you will stand in its path and turn your face to it and open your life to its influence."[13]

Another sample shows his brilliance with the paradox he finds in Luke 3:1-2:

"In the fifteenth year of the reign of Caesar, in the governorship of Pontius Pilate"—how solid and influential and enduring it seemed, that drama of the nations—"the word of God came to John in the wilderness"—how trivial and evanescent, by comparison, that! But history itself has given the verdict. Tiberius,

Pilate, Herod, Lysanias, and all their pomp and might—mere foam on the face of time's hurrying stream: but John, the called of God, standing foursquare still to the winds of the centuries, standing like that very Rock of Ages to whom all his words bore witness!

What a contrast it is between the passing and the permanent; between lives that go out like a candle when they are done . . . and lives that go marching on deathlessly for ever, because they are eternal with the very eternity of God![14]

Implications

The reading of good literature is important not least for the appreciation of language and for direct application in preaching. In the Nicodemus passage, Stewart displays great language and narrative skill in compressing many pieces of information. In the second sentence alone we learn that it is night, there is at least a half-moon, there is scattered cloud, a strong wind is blowing, Jesus and Nicodemus are facing Jerusalem, and the city can be seen, illumined by the moon, which is directly above. Some of these details are amplified or reinforced, as they need to be, in the sentences that follow, all of which contribute to the enormous richness of his prose. We do not need separate sentences or phrases for each detail we wish to communicate, and it is often better if many of our sentences can achieve several basic objectives at once (things like who? where? why? what? when?).

Note the liberties that Stewart takes with his text. Luke never mentions the location, or the moon, or even that a wind is actually blowing, nor does he attribute to Nicodemus a sense "of failure and emptiness." The latter is known as psychologizing the text, attributing to a character psychological motivation for which there is no actual basis in the text. (We know Nicodemus came to Jesus for a reason the text does not provide. We also know that we might seek Jesus out of failure. But we do not know this of Nicodemus, nor is the text concerned with his motive.) The principle Stewart seems to be following is that freedom may be taken once the essential meaning of the text has been ensured for the sermon. Our dilemma is worthy: We need to balance being true to the text (i.e., not psychologizing) with a refusal to present it as a dusty document.

There is a wonderful sense of mystery in Stewart's preaching that is lacking in much preaching today. He seems to have two related sources we might tap: One is the mystery that is produced by use of apparent opposites or paradoxes to communicate truth, as in the last sample quoted (the solid is mere foam, while the seemingly trivial is permanent). Opposites may be used not just in poignant phrases or in paragraphs that probe the poles. They may be used in following the structure of thesis-antithesis-synthesis.

The second source of mystery arises from his stress on exalting Christ in every sermon and testing each sermon by asking whether the congregation met God. The central paradox of his sermons is the paradox of the cross and resurrection. Each of us might attempt Stewart's fourfold recommendation for preaching Christ and his threefold suggestion for preaching the cross, mentioned earlier, in order to help us articulate what we ourselves believe. As Stewart said, we cannot proclaim something unless we are possessed by it.[15] There is nothing to prevent focus on the cross from being combined with social analysis and criticism, even though he did not himself do it.

In many churches it is now unusual to have Sunday morning and evening services, with preaching at each. Stewart recommended Wednesday night as the deadline for preparing the first one and Friday night for the second. He understood the importance of time for excellence in composition. This means not simply allowing sufficient time for study of the text and for reading in diverse areas including literature. It also means allowing sufficient time for images, ideas, and phrases to mature and ripen. Extending preparation over many days is one of the best ways to see an immediate improvement in preaching. Why not set Wednesday as a deadline, even if we preach only one sermon on Sundays? We could then use short periods of time on the remaining days to revise, rethink, rewrite, and to absorb our material as we prepare to deliver it. We might even start work on the sermon for the next Sunday, to allow ten days for germination.

CHAPTER 20

Martin Luther King, Jr. (1929–1968)
Black Baptist—the
Authority of the Oppressed

Martin Luther King, Jr., did not grow up in the dire poverty of his father's sharecropping family. His father had become a country preacher at age fifteen, and then went to Atlanta, Georgia, where he put himself through high school and divinity studies at Morehouse College. He married the daughter of the pastor at Ebenezer Baptist Church, and shortly after M. L. (his nickname throughout life) was born, his father took over as pastor of that church.

Abraham Lincoln's Emancipation Proclamation of 1863 and the end of the Civil War resulted in the slaves being freed, but they had no land, few means, and no real equality. The South that King came to know with intimacy was a place of prejudice and injustice, completely segregated in all aspects of life. Racial violence was openly promoted by the Ku Klux Klan (from the Greek *kuklos* = "circle" and "clan"), a group formed by unemployed Confederate troops in 1866 who originally protested carpetbaggers but soon moved to terrorize the new black voters. Churches became the center of black community life. King's own initial denomination emerged from post–Civil War black Baptist churches that associated to form the National Baptist Convention of

America and, after a split in 1916, the National Baptist Convention, U.S.A.

Successive scholarships took King from Morehouse (B.A.), to Crozer Seminary (B.D.) near Philadelphia, where he learned of Mahatma Gandhi, to Boston University (Ph.D.). While in Boston he married Coretta Scott. He became frustrated with the gradualism of the "Social Gospel" in its pursuit of human progress and was put off by the totality of human sin that he found expressed in neoorthodoxy. When they returned to the South in 1954, this time for him to pastor in Montgomery, Alabama, he brought to the civil rights movement not just his strong faith, but also Gandhi's idea of *satyagraha*—nonviolent resistance based on commitment to both justice and love for the oppressor. In December 1955, he was thrust to national prominence by leading the thirteen-month boycott of that city's segregated transit system, first sparked by Rosa Parks' refusal to give up her seat to a white person. He spoke with eloquence and artful rhetoric: "We have sometimes given our white brothers the feeling that we liked the way we were being treated. But we come here tonight to be saved from that patience that makes us patient with anything less than freedom and justice."[1]

In spite of his own home being bombed, he persisted and with Ralph Abernathy organized the Southern Christian Leadership Conference to spearhead successive civil rights campaigns primarily in the South and in Chicago. His famous address, "I Have a Dream," was delivered in the Washington march in 1963, three years after he had moved to co-pastor with his father at Ebenezer Baptist Church. In 1964, the same year that the Civil Rights Act enforced desegregation and rejected discrimination, he was awarded the Nobel Peace Prize. The day before his death in Memphis, Tennessee, from an assassin's bullet on April 4, 1968, he spoke of having been "to the mountaintop. . . . and I've seen the Promised Land." By then his concerns had broadened to include housing, poverty, and the Vietnam War. The underlying world problem was not the communist threat, he said, it was the difference between rich and poor. He advocated elimination of poverty in America through universal employment opportunities and adequate guaranteed annual income. He came to believe, at the cost of much popularity, that society could not be reformed; it had to be restructured through a nonviolent moral revolution.

King was driven to his positions by his conscience as "a preacher," and he used his frequent preaching to further his causes. He wrote several books including a sermon collection, *Strength to Love* (1963). When he died, he had been awarded more than twenty honorary degrees from around the world.

Homiletical Setting

King's preaching has its roots in the black oral tradition of heartfelt religion that has been described by writers like James E. Massey (*Designing the Sermon*, 1980), Henry H. Mitchell (*Black Preaching*, 1990; *Celebration and Experience in Preaching*, 1990), Bruce Rosenberg (*The Art of the American Folk-Preacher*, 1970), and Richard Lischer.[2] Some general features may have parallels in the folk-preaching traditions of other cultures and in early church preaching like that of Romanos the Melodist. These features include:

1) The "cognitive" purpose is produced in the sermon by the controlling idea and by the need to demonstrate the truth of ideas. This is secondary, however, to the "emotive" purpose, which is to affect the lives of the congregation. Material is chosen, says Mitchell, according to its "affective purpose," and it is the "emotional logic," or

what might be called an evidence of the Holy Spirit, which must prevail.

2) Sermons are constructed to take account of musical features in language, often starting slowly with long sentences, working to faster-paced rhythmical grouping of words, sometimes chanted ("intoned," "moaned"), and ascending to a final climax of joy or celebration of the victory that God is accomplishing. The sermon is filled with hope. It may move into an altar call. The rhythmic and rhyming patterns of language have often been imprinted on the preacher's mind from childhood exposure to the church.

3) The congregation is part of the sermon delivery, and the preacher depends upon their energy and response. This response is usually led by elders using short phrases that communicate things like timing, how the sermon is being received, when a point needs emphasis or development, and when the preacher should end. The responses might come in the form of humming, yelling, singing aloud—all well-timed. The purpose of this communal activity in preaching is to help the people "feel" the truth sufficiently such that they want to enact it.

4) The preacher's use of set phrases and short rhetorical formulas, which the congregation may recognize, is expected, as well as the recycling of familiar portions of earlier sermons, sometimes as set-pieces. Use of fine ideas and phrases from unnamed other preachers is also honored.

5) Vivid details and powerful images and symbols are preferred to syllogisms.

6) The black experience of *poverty, suffering,* and *oppression* is the prism through which Scripture is read, and the backdrop for all that is said. Scripture is generally accepted at face value. It is often reworked, sometimes using narrative to retell the biblical stories.

7) The values embedded in the founding documents of

the United States are upheld in the black Christian hope for America.

Richard Lischer listened to tapes of King's sermons. He makes these observations more specifically of King:

1) Many of the sermons in *Strength to Love* are polished versions of sermons repeated and reworked from graduate school. They have been "decontextualized" and contain nothing of the extemporaneous and "scarcely a memory of his voice."[3]

2) On audiotape, a King sermon typically shows his fatigue at the beginning. It proceeds, "with a relentless monotony, until the preacher is awakened to the urgency of his own message. The pace quickens, the diction becomes more effusive, images begin to flower, and suddenly [it] becomes one of the most exciting compositions you have ever heard."[4]

3) His sermons are so linked with the civil rights movement that they generally offer the opportunity of a "focused response": either moving the people out into the streets, or reshaping black consciousness and attitudes.[5]

Sermon Sample

The following is a "set-piece" not found in published versions of his sermons:

Oh there will be a day. The question won't be how many awards did you get in life. Not that day. It won't be how popular were ya in your social setting. That won't be the question that day. It will not ask how many degrees you've been able to get. The question that day will not be concerned whether you are a Ph.D or a No.D, will not be concerned whether you went to Morehouse or . . . No House. . . . On that day the question will be what did you do for others. Now I can hear somebody saying, "Lord, uh, I did a lot of things in life. I did my job well . . . I did a lot of things Lord, I went to school and studied hard. I accumulated a lot of money, Lord, that's what I did." Seems as if I can hear the Lord of Light saying, "But I was hungry, and you fed me not. I was sick and ye visited me not. I was *neck*-id in the cold, and I was in prison and you weren't concerned about me, so get out of my face!"[6]

The next extract is from the climax of King's last Christmas Eve sermon, broadcast nationally in Canada by CBC Radio and published as the fifth of his Massey lectures. His biblical text is three words, "Peace on Earth." He echoes his 1963 Washington speech:

Today over 500,000 American boys are fighting on Asian soil. Yes, I am personally the victim of deferred dreams, of blasted hopes, but in spite of that I close today by saying I still have a dream, because, you know, you can't give up in life. If you lose hope, somehow you lose that vitality that keeps life moving, you lose that courage to be, that quality that helps you to go on in spite of all. And so today I still have a dream.

I have a dream that one day men will rise up and come to see that they are made to live together as brothers. I still have a dream this morning that one day every Negro in this country, every colored person in the world, will be judged on the basis of the content of his character rather than the color of his skin, and every man will respect the dignity and worth of human personality. I still have a dream today that one day the idle industries of Appalachia will be revitalized, and the empty stomachs of Mississippi will be filled, and brotherhood will be more than a few words at the end of a prayer, but rather the first order of business on every legislative agenda. I still have a dream today that one day justice will roll down like water, and righteousness like a mighty stream. I still have a dream today. . . . that one day every valley shall be exalted and every mountain and hill will be made low, the rough places will be made smooth and the crooked places straight, and the glory of the Lord shall be revealed, and all flesh shall see it together. I still have a dream that with this faith we will be able to adjourn the councils of despair and bring new light into the dark chambers of pessimism. With this faith we will be able to speed up the day when there will be peace on earth and goodwill toward men. It will be a glorious day, the morning stars will sing together, and the sons of God will shout for joy.[7]

Implications

African-American preaching that has its roots in oral culture is one of the most powerful forms of preaching today. Set-pieces are only one aspect of its power. They create a response in the people because the people recognize the familiar and expect to participate. In the first selection quoted, there is a playfulness, generated in part by the use of street language and in part by the slow movement and the "set-up," which is like that of a good joke. Four times the question is mentioned. Three times the response comes back, each time slightly altered: ("Lord, I did a lot of things. . . . I did a lot of things Lord. . . . Lord, that's what I did"). But it is not all play, as the surprising "punch line" at the end indicates. It is a good homiletical use of humor and playfulness that does not forget serious intent.

In the second passage quoted, we may note several things: the revision of his famous format; the echo between "Vietnam" and his own "blasted hopes"; Paul Tillich's title "The Courage to Be"; the strong, vibrant hope that keeps pulsing through his words; the manner in which the biblical materials are woven into the fabric of his message; and the striking use of vivid images like "adjourn the councils of despair" and "the dark chambers of pessimism," instead of just saying "despair and pessimism."

For those of us who would like more rhythm in parts of our own sermons, we might try writing with that in mind, remembering the way King's sermons sound. To prepare, we can go through King's words and line them out as poetry. This form of writing might also assist the memory:

> I still have a dream
> that one day men will rise up
> and come to see
> that they are made to live together as brothers.
> I still have a dream this morning
> that one day every Negro in this country,
> every colored person in this world,
> will be judged
> on the basis of the content of his character,
> rather than the color of his skin,
> and every man
> will respect the dignity and worth of human personality.

Most preachers have at some point longed for the kind of congregational involvement in preaching that many African American preachers receive. If the culture of those congregations is not our own, we cannot expect it, at least in the same ways. But we can provide what is the foundation of any real involvement and what King did so well: Anticipate the needs, speak to the issues, call on the good traditions out of which we come, pay attention to enhancing the natural music in words and speech, and bring a strong and energetic message of hope founded in the one God who reigns through all time.

CONCLUSION

The concise study we have made of the history of preaching is of course too short. To examine only twenty preachers out of thousands leaves a path perhaps remarkable mainly for what has been missed. But the purpose here was to give as much of a taste as is possible in a few pages, to awaken the historical palate, and to encourage us all to learn further from our preaching past for our preaching today.

We may identify three broad fields that seem to have been of particular assistance to preachers: biblical studies, theology, and language and art. Puritan "plain style" preaching notwithstanding, with its ostensible emphasis on exposition, preaching has rarely plumbed the exegetical depths of the text, even in our own century. In our sample of preachers, at least, many of the sermons of the church fathers and of Luther and Calvin remain biblically the most thorough. It is not surprising that the most biblical sermons seem to come from those preachers who were involved in writing commentaries.

It may be surprising that Protestant elevation of the Word seems to have had its primary impact on the worship service and on Bible study in various settings—home, church, and school. It did not generally result in making the individual biblical text in itself an object of particular homiletical attachment or devotion, or in generating for the sermon the biblical text as a historical text to be opened and explored. Rather, the individual text generally continues to function as it did, as a source for a theme of exposition that may have something to do with the text's meaning, and to which any number of other texts may be brought to serve as reinforcements.

The relative lack of direct impact of biblical criticism on preaching, with notable exceptions, at least until our present decades with increased ecumenical focus on the lectionary, poses some intriguing possibilities for us. It suggests, for instance, that the histories of biblical criticism apply less to conversations in the church at large than they do to interchanges between a select number of scholars. There may be chapters of the history of biblical criticism that need to be rewritten, if the actual preaching of the church is to be explored and included in them. Perhaps in this regard we need to be rethinking openly what is the link between scholarly pursuit and the life of the church.

Another possibility has to do with our own understanding of the proclamation of the Word as being tied to the actual words and meanings of biblical verses in context. This is a much narrower understanding than we have seen put to actual practice in the small sample of preachers examined here. The predominant view of scriptural interpretation that is gained from looking at sermons suggests that the understanding of biblical "text" has generally been different from our own. "Text" seems to imply the entire canon of Scripture, not individual units or pericopes with their own individual meanings and histories. One of the common tendencies of modern preaching is to preach histories of texts, or to preach the commentaries, instead of preaching to the faith needs of the community. Perhaps in our own important pursuit of the meaning of individual texts, we need to hold onto the broader understanding of "text as entire canon," such that we do not lose sight of both its dangers and its benefits.

A second source of homiletical ferment, related to the first, has been theological inquiry. This is particularly true of those preachers who forced themselves or were forced by their times to rethink the doctrines they had inherited. Augustine, as well as many of the other excellent preachers we have seen, wrote in order to discover what he thought. It cannot be stressed sufficiently that if we want to be excellent preachers in our own day, the route cannot be separate from study. There is simply no substitute, particularly in an age when many of our people are themselves highly educated. Many of the great books in theology, with the exception of most in modern times, have been written by preachers pursuing great causes first in their sermons and then in revised versions for book manuscripts. To the advantage of these books, they arose from the setting of congregational life.

A third source of homiletical ferment, which cannot be entirely separated from the previous two, has been the study of language and art, rhetorical or otherwise. We have seen sermonic form become more obvious and self-conscious, with increased attention to matters belonging to the ancient rhetorical canon of Arrangement, in the Middle Ages and beyond. Many preachers have also demonstrated great sensitivity to language and to the sermon as a form of art: Augustine, Romanos, Donne, Bushnell, Stewart, and King are clear examples. At the same time few preachers until our current age have spent much time proportionally on Jesus' form of art—on his parables as opposed to his sayings and actions. One reason for this may have been the relative difficulty of reducing the parables to a number of points.

We have also seen the increasing authority in language of metaphor and paradox. This originally stems from people like Origen, who read all Scripture symbolically, sometimes in ludicrous fashion, and who established a long and tortuous tradition of allegorical interpretation.

A strong shift occurred in the Reformation, for two reasons. First, there was general popular acceptance of the medieval scholastic notion of "analogy," particularly the "analogy of being"—that is, the idea that the material world contains analogies of the divine world. Analogy (which implies "like") rather than allegory (which implies one-to-one correspondence or "identity") became a common way of thought.

Second, analogy allowed for a reappropriation of allegory, which, in the hands of people like John Donne and Jonathan Edwards, is no longer an absolute statement about the true meaning of Scripture. Allegory begins to function like analogy, symbol, or metaphor. This was further shaped by people like Bushnell and in our time by various studies of symbol, metaphor, parable, myth, and narrative. Rather than there existing an authoritative interpretation sought in Cyprian's day, the biblical text has come to have a plurality of meanings, any number of which may be authenticated by our faith traditions.

We have seen other themes:

1) With few exceptions the Protestant preachers here have used a version of the law-gospel dialectic, stressing the importance of both naming sin and preaching hope. We first found this in Paul and in Augustine's emphasis on the rule of love and the primacy of grace. It was given explicit renewed theological emphasis, particularly by Luther and Wesley.

2) The early church idea of the word as sound was lost in the Middle Ages when the idea of the word became private text. Luther recovered the early church emphasis. But Luther could not stop his own preached word from appearing as a text in print, without his authorization, shortly after he descended from the pulpit. Currently we seem to need it both ways: We call any speech or discourse a text (implying a written document) even as we

have trouble calling a written text a sermon if it has not actually been preached (implying an oral speech). We are now in the process of recovering the importance of shaping the sermon according to the aural needs of the congregation.

3) The early church idea of the word as unit of meaning shifted around the time of Luther and the printing press. The sentence became the unit of meaning, even as today it sometimes seems to become the entire pericope.

4) We have seen variations in the function of experience in the sermon (Augustine and Calvin in practice excluded it); and in the use of narrative and music.

5) We have seen Jesus' bias toward the poor extend from Chrysostom through the mendicant preaching orders particularly to Wesley, Booth, and King.

6) We have seen the evangelical tradition of Wesley and others hold together individual piety and social justice. At various places along the way, and not least in the time of Stewart, many mainline churches lost their evangelical enthusiasm or transferred it to their pursuit of social justice, even as many evangelical churches were distracted from social justice in the pursuit of the individual soul.

7) We have also seen the Protestant focus on the individual relationship to God move from the Calvinistic concern with commonwealth, to the adoption of progress as a religious paradigm, to Fosdick's (and to some degree our own) preoccupation with both progress and individual psychological motivation.

Why stop where we have? To go much beyond takes us out of the realm of history and into current experience, which, in its own due time, will be a fascinating chapter of the preaching tradition, not least because of the number of women in ordained ministries. We are now witnessing developments on a number of fronts. We are participating in a development in our society that will prove to be as eventful as the discovery of the printing press. Once again we are becoming a largely oral culture shaped this time by the popular media (Walter J. Ong has called this "second stage orality") and personal computers. The way we think is being altered on subjects like attention span, use of imagery, and length and manner of discourse, quite apart from issues posed by televangelism and multi-media sermons.

Today many preachers are making greater use of narrative. Biblical study and higher criticism are playing more of a role in preaching. This has been influenced by Vatican II, which saw a recovery of preaching for the Catholic mass, but also resulted, in North America at least, in the ecumenical sharing of a three-year lectionary. Roman Catholic and Protestant study resources are being exchanged freely. With the movement for liturgical reform in many denominations, we are seeing a recovery of the Christian year and of the link between Word and Table. More music, more readings of Scripture, more prayers, more frequent celebration of communion, are putting pressure on preachers to cut sermons short, much shorter than the consistent norm of an hour we have found in this study. This has profound implications for our theology of the word. More focus on the lectionary also implies less opportunity for thematic or doctrinal preaching, at least as we have come to know these.

History will need to be the judge of some of these developments. It is both a challenging and an exciting time to be a preacher. But then, as one looks back over the centuries, one is struck that preachers in good times and in bad have always experienced the privilege it is to proclaim God's Word, empowered by the Holy Spirit.

NOTES

INTRODUCTION

1. Yngve Brilioth, *A Brief History of Preaching* (Fortress Press, 1965).
2. Tom Harper, "Ethics: Proof Positive Early Church Had Women Priests," *The Toronto Star*, January 5, 1992.
3. Fabienne Nitro-Garriga, "Saint Geneviève, patronne de Paris" in *Notre histoire: La mémoire religieuse de l'humanité* 86 (February 1992): 24-36.
4. Abingdon Press, 1996.

I. THE EARLY CHURCH: THE AUTHORITY OF THE WORD AS SOUND

1. Isaac Levy, *The Synagogue: Its History and Function* (London: Vallentine Press, 1963), p. 102.
2. In Hugh T. Kerr, ed., *Readings in Christian Thought*, 2nd ed. (Nashville: Abingdon Press, 1990), p. 20.
3. See *Orality and Literacy* (Methuen, 1982).

CHAPTER 1: THE PRE-GOSPELS AND PAUL: THE NEW TESTAMENT AS PREACHING

1. *See* Gerd Theissen, *The First Followers of Jesus* (London: S.C.M. Press, 1978).
2. Cited by Edgar J. Goodspeed, *A History of Early Christian Literature* (Chicago: University of Chicago Press, 1942), p. 2.
3. Reprinted from *Rhetoric and the New Testament* by Burton L. Mack (Minneapolis: Fortress Press, 1990), pp. 56-57. Copyright © 1990 Augsburg Fortress. Used by permission.
4. Ibid., p. 55.
5. Thomas G. Long, *Preaching the Literary Forms of the Gospels* (Philadelphia: Westminster Press, 1989).
6. Raymond Bailey, *Jesus the Preacher* and *Paul the Preacher* (Nashville: Broadman Press, 1990, 1991). *See also* Robin Scroggs, "Paul as Rhetorician: Two Homilies in Romans 1–11" in Robert Hamerton-Kelly and Robin Scroggs, eds., *Jews, Greeks, and Christians* (Leiden: E. J. Brill, 1976), pp. 271-97.

7. *See* Paul Scott Wilson, *Imagination of the Heart: New Understandings in Preaching* (Nashville: Abingdon Press, 1988).

CHAPTER 2: PERPETUA (c. 181–203): MARTYRDOM AS THE HIGHEST FORM OF WITNESS

1. Hugh T. Kerr, *Readings in Christian Thought*, 2nd ed. (Nashville: Abingdon Press, 1990), pp. 23-24.
2. Herbert Musurillo, *The Acts of the Christian Martyrs* (New York: Oxford University Press, 1972), p. 59.
3. Ibid., pp. 109-14.
4. Ibid., p. 111.
5. *The "I" of the Sermon* (Fortress Press, 1990).

CHAPTER 3: ORIGEN (185–254): ALEXANDRIA AND ALLEGORY

1. *See* Joseph Wilson Trigg, *Origen* (Atlanta: John Knox Press, 1983), esp. pp. 176-88; and Joseph T. Lienhard, S.J., "Origen as Homilist" in David G. Hunter, ed., *Preaching in the Patristic Age* (New York: Paulist Press, 1989), pp. 36-52.
2. Maurice Wiles and Mark Santer, eds., *Documents in Early Christian Thought* (Cambridge: Cambridge University Press, 1975), pp. 7-10.

CHAPTER 4: CHRYSOSTOM (c. 347–407): ANTIOCH AND THE LITERAL

1. Henry Chadwick, *The Early Church* (London: Penguin Books Ltd., 1967), p. 191 n. 1.
2. For a more complete treatment of Rabbi Hillel's first-century hermeneutics, *see* Louis Jacobs, "Hermeneutics," in *Encyclopaedia Judaica* (New York: Macmillan, 1971), cols. 367-72.
3. Chrysostom, "On the Statues," Homily 4:5, in *Nicene and Post-Nicene Fathers of the Christian Church*, vol. 9 (New York: Christian Literature Co., 1889).
4. Chrysostom, "On I Corinthians," Homily 9:1-2, in Maurice Wiles and Mark Santer, eds., *Documents in Early Christian Thought* (Cambridge: Cambridge University Press, 1975), pp. 253-54.

CHAPTER 5: ROMANOS THE MELODIST (c. 490–c. 560): CONSTANTINOPLE AND POETRY

1. *See* Joseph R. Jeters, Jr., "A Development of Poetic Preaching: A Slice of History," in *Homiletic* 15 (Winter 1990): 5-12. Jeters considers the metrical homily tradition with particular reference to Ephraim, Romanos, and John of Damascus.
2. *See* Egon Wellesz, *A History of Byzantine Music and Hymnography* (Oxford: Clarendon Press, 1961), pp. 48ff.

3. Reprinted from *Kontakia of Romanos: Byzantine Melodist I*, trans. Marjorie Carpenter, by permission of the University of Missouri Press. Copyright © 1970 by the Curators of the University of Missouri (Columbia, Mo.: University of Missouri Press, 1970, 1973), vol. 1, pp. 40-41.

CHAPTER 6: CYPRIAN (200–258): CARTHAGE AND AUTHORITATIVE EXEGESIS

1. *See* Robert M. Grant with David Tracy, "The Authoritative Interpretation," in their *Short History of the Interpretation of the Bible*, 2nd ed. (Minneapolis: Fortress Press, 1984), pp. 73-82.
2. *See* Michael Fahey, *Cyprian and the Bible: A Study in Third-Century Exegesis* (Tubingen: J. C. B. Hohr, 1970), esp. pp. 46-56.
3. Alexander Roberts and James Donaldson, eds., *The Ante-Nicene Fathers*, vol. 5 (Buffalo: Christian Literature Co., 1886), p. 448.
4. Ibid., p. 449.

CHAPTER 7: AUGUSTINE (354–430): HIPPO AND THE PRIMACY OF THE RULE OF LOVE

1. *On Christian Doctrine*, trans. D. W. Robinson, Jr. (Indianapolis: Bobbs-Merrill Co., 1958).
2. *St. Augustine: Sermons for Christmas and Epiphany*, trans. Thomas Comerford Lawler (Westminster, Md.: Newman Press, 1952).

II. THE MIDDLE AGES: THE AUTHORITY OF THE WORD AS PRIVATE TEXT

1. Quoted in Robert E. McNally, S.J., *The Bible in the Early Middle Ages* (Westminster, Md.: Newman Press, 1959), p. 13.
2. In A. Berkeley Mickelsen, *Interpreting the Bible* (Grand Rapids, Mich.: Wm. B. Eerdmans Publishing Co., 1963), p. 35.
3. *See* Richard Lischer, *Theories of Preaching: Selected Readings in the Homiletical Tradition* (Durham, N.C.: Labyrinth Press, 1987), pp. 9-13.
4. Ibid., p. 220.

CHAPTER 8: HILDEGARD OF BINGEN (1098–1179): THE WORD OF THE SPIRIT

1. From *St. Benedict's Rule* (chap. 24) in Robert E. McNally, S.J., *The Bible in the Early Middle Ages*, p. 12.
2. Caroline Walker Bynum, "Preface," in *Hildegard of Bingen: Scivias*, Columba Hart and Jane Bishop, trans. (Mahwah, N.J.: Paulist Press, 1990), p. 5.
3. In Gabriele Uhlein, O.S.F., *Meditations with Hildegard of Bingen* (Sante Fe: Bear and Co., 1983), p. 49.
4. Quoted and trans. Sabina Flanagan, *Hildegard of Bingen, 1098–1179:*

A Visionary Life (New York: Routledge, 1990), pp. 174-75. From P. Migne, "S. Hildegardis" in *Patrologiae Cursus Completus,* vol. 197 (Paris: 1882), pp. 243-44.

5. Hart and Bishop, *Hildegard of Bingen,* I, 4:29, p. 87.

CHAPTER 9: THOMAS AQUINAS (c. 1225–1274): THE WORD OF REASON

1. From *Summa theologica,* I, Q. 1, Art. 10, in Aquinas, *Nature and Grace,* A. M. Fairweather, trans., vol. 11, *The Library of Christian Classics* (Philadelphia: Westminster Press, 1954), p. 49.

2. John M. Ashley, trans., *Ninety-Nine Homilies of S. Thomas Aquinas* (London: Church Press Co., 1867), pp. 3ff.

III. THE REFORMATIONS: THE AUTHORITY OF THE COMMON TEXT

CHAPTER 10: MARTIN LUTHER (1483–1546): LUTHERAN PROTESTANT—THE AUTHORITY OF LAW AND GOSPEL

1. Quoted in Fred W. Meuser and Stanley D. Schneider, eds., *Interpreting Luther's Legacy* (Minneapolis: Augsburg, 1969), pp. 19, 30.

2. Quoted by Yngve Brilioth, *A Brief History of Preaching,* trans. Karl E. Mattson (Philadelphia: Fortress Press, 1965), p. 113.

3. *Luther's Works,* vol. 51, "Sermons I," ed. and trans. John W. Doberstein (Philadelphia: Muhlenburg Press, 1959), pp. 278-81.

4. Ibid., p. 99.

5. *See* Gerhard O. Forde, *Theology Is for Proclamation* (Minneapolis: Fortress Press, 1990), pp. 150ff.; and Paul Scott Wilson, *Imagination of the Heart: New Understandings in Preaching* (Nashville: Abingdon Press, 1988), pp. 91ff.

6. For a discussion of Luther's "unpreached" God, see Forde, *Theology,* pp. 13ff.

CHAPTER 11: JOHN CALVIN (1509–1564): REFORMED PROTESTANT—THE AUTHORITY OF CORRECTION

1. T. H. L. Parker, *The Oracles of God: An Introduction to the Preaching of John Calvin* (London: Lutterworth Press, 1947), pp. 70-71.

2. I am indebted in these two paragraphs to William J. Bouwsma, *John Calvin, A Sixteenth-Century Portrait* (New York: Oxford University Press, 1988), pp. 99-109, 118-27.

3. John Calvin, "The Proper Use of Scripture," in *The Mystery of Godliness and Other Selected Sermons* (Grand Rapids, Mich.: Wm. B. Eerdmans Publishing Co., 1950), pp. 135-36.

4. William K. McElvaney, *Preaching from Camelot to Covenant: Announc-*

ing God's Action in the World (Nashville: Abingdon Press, 1989), esp. pp. 19-41. *See also* Arthur Van Seters, ed., *Preaching as a Social Act: Theology and Practice* (Nashville: Abingdon Press, 1988); and James W. Crawford, *Worthy to Raise Issues: Preaching and Public Responsibility* (Cleveland: Pilgrim Press, 1991).

CHAPTER 12: JOHN DONNE (1572–1631): ANGLICAN PROTESTANT—THE AUTHORITY OF METAPHYSICAL HOPE

1. Horton Davies, *Like Angels from a Cloud: The English Metaphysical Preachers (1588–1645)* (San Marino, Calif.: Huntington Library, 1986).
2. Cited by Walter R. Davis, "Meditation, Typology, and Sermons," in Claude J. Summers and Ted-Larry Pebworth, eds., *The Eagle and the Dove: Reassessing John Donne* (Columbia, Mo.: University of Missouri Press, 1986), p. 173.
3. Izaak Walton, quoted in R. Bald, *John Donne: A Life* (Oxford: Oxford at the Clarendon Press, 1970), p. 406.
4. John Donne, *Devotions Upon Emergent Occasions*, ed. Anthony Raspa (New York: Oxford University Press, 1987), pp. 99, 100.
5. Ibid., p. 87.
6. John Donne, *The Sermons of John Donne*, ed. Evelyn M. Simpson and George R. Potter, 10 vols. (Berkeley, Calif.: University of California Press, 1953–62), vol. 9, pp. 127-28.

CHAPTER 13: ALPHONSUS LIGUORI (1696–1787): REDEMPTORIST—THE AUTHORITY OF THE TERRIBLE MORAL

1. *The Complete Works of Saint Alphonsus de Liguori*, vol. 15, "Preaching," trans. Rev. Eugene Grimm (New York: Benziger Brothers, 1890), 584 pp. Charles Grandison Finney (1792–1875) would later devise from the Protestant perspective a similarly detailed strategy that would provide the blueprint for evangelical revivals even to the current day. *See* his *Lectures on the Revivals of Religion* [1835], William G. McLoughlin, ed. (Repr. Cambridge: Belknap Press of Harvard University Press, 1960).
2. *See* sermons 5 and 7 in Alphonsus M. Liguori, *Sermons Upon Various Subjects*, trans. anon. (Dublin: Richard Grace, Catholic Bookseller, 1845), pp. 59ff., 84ff.
3. *The Sermons of St. Alphonsus Liguori for All Sundays of the Year* [1852], trans. anon. (Repr. Rockford, Ill.: Tan Books and Publishers, 1982), pp. 94-95.

CHAPTER 14: JONATHAN EDWARDS (1703–1758): CONGREGATIONAL—THE AUTHORITY OF EXPERIENCE, AND THE PROMISED LAND

1. *See* Stephen J. Stein, ed., "Editor's Introduction," in Jonathan Edwards, *Apocalyptic Writings* (New Haven: Yale University Press, 1977), pp. 15ff.
2. *See* John F. Wilson, ed., "Editor's Introduction," in Jonathan Edwards, *A History of the Work of Redemption* (New Haven: Yale University Press, 1989), pp. 40ff., esp. p. 66, regarding images.
3. H. Norman Gardiner, *Selected Sermons of Jonathan Edwards* (New York: Macmillan, 1904), p. 88.
4. Wilson, *A History of the Work,* pp. 434-35.

CHAPTER 15: JOHN WESLEY (1703–1791): METHODIST—THE AUTHORITY OF LAW AND GOSPEL

1. W. L. Doughty, *John Wesley: Preacher* (London: Epworth Press, 1955), p. 6.
2. *See* Albert C. Outler, ed., *John Wesley* (New York: Oxford University Press, 1964), pp. 232-37.
3. These are published most recently in vols. 1 to 4 of *The Works of John Wesley* (Abingdon Press, 1984–87) and in *John Wesley's Sermons: An Anthology* (Abingdon Press, 1991).
4. *See* Doughty, *John Wesley: Preacher,* pp. 107ff.
5. John Wesley, *The Works of John Wesley,* vol. 1, Sermons I, 1-33, ed. Albert C. Outler (Nashville: Abingdon Press, 1984), pp. 198-99.
6. Henry H. Mitchell, *Celebration and Experience in Preaching* (Nashville: Abingdon Press, 1990).

CHAPTER 16: HORACE BUSHNELL (1802–1876): CONGREGATIONAL—THE AUTHORITY OF IMAGINATION

1. *See* Horace Bushnell, *Forgiveness and Law, Grounded in Principles Interpreted by Human Analogies* (New York: Scribner, Armstrong, & Co., 1874), pp. 120ff.
2. Horace Bushnell, "Preliminary Dissertation on the Nature of Language as Related to Thought and Spirit," extracts in H. Shelton Smith, ed., *Horace Bushnell* (New York: Oxford University Press, 1965), pp. 89, 98-99. Also, in Horace Bushnell, *God in Christ* (Hartford: Brown and Parsons, 1849), pp. 43, 72ff.
3. Horace Bushnell, "The Coronation of the Lamb," in *Sermons on Living Subjects* (New York: Charles Scribner's Sons, 1897), esp. pp. 426ff.
4. *See* Horace Bushnell, *Forgiveness and Law,* pp. 120-33ff.
5. Horace Bushnell, "Our Gospel, a Gift to the Imagination" in Con-

rad Cherry, ed., *Horace Bushnell: Sermons* (New York: Paulist Press, 1985), pp. 95-117, esp. p. 109.

6. Horace Bushnell, "Preliminary Dissertation on the Nature of Language " (1965), pp. 93-94; (1849), p. 55.

7. Bushnell, "Our Gospel," p. 100.

8. Ibid., p. 99.

9. Ibid., p. 101.

10. In Horace Bushnell, *The Vicarious Sacrifice* (London: Richard D. Dickinson, 1880), pp. 451-76.

11. Ibid., p. 471.

12. Ibid., p. 454.

13. Ibid., pp. 455ff.

14. Ibid., p. 471.

15. Ibid., p. 459.

16. Ibid., p. 460.

17. Ibid., p. 461.

18. *Christ and His Salvation* (London: Richard D. Dickenson, 1880), pp. 3-6.

CHAPTER 17: CATHERINE MUMFORD BOOTH (1829–1890): SALVATION ARMY—THE AUTHORITY OF "AGGRESSION"

1. *See* David Albert Farmer and Edwina Hunter, *And Blessed Is She: Sermons by Women* (San Francisco: Harper and Row, 1990).

2. Both letters are quoted in Cyril Barnes, *Words of Catherine Booth* (London: Salvationist Publishing and Supplies, 1981), pp. 10, 12.

3. *The Salvation Army in Relation to the Church and State* (London: Salvation Army, 1883).

4. Ibid., p. 31.

5. Ibid., p. 41.

6. Ibid., p. 53.

7. *Papers on Aggressive Christianity* (London: Salvation Army, 1891), p. 164.

8. *Papers on Practical Religion* (London: Salvation Army, 1891), pp. 195-96.

9. *Church and State*, p. 39.

10. *Godliness* (London: Salvation Army, 1883), pp. 15ff.

11. *Life and Death* (London: Salvation Army, 1890), pp. 83ff.

12. Ibid., p. 33.

13. *Practical Religion*, p. 3.

14. *Aggressive Christianity*, p. 176.

15. *Godliness*, p. 120.

16. Anne Bemrose-Fetter in a preaching class in the Toronto School of Theology, 1992.

CHAPTER 18: HARRY EMERSON FOSDICK (1878–1969): BAPTIST—THE AUTHORITY OF PASTORAL COUNSELING

1. In Lionel Crocker, ed., *Harry Emerson Fosdick's Art of Preaching: An Anthology* (Springfield, Ill.: Charles C. Thomas, Publisher, 1971), p. 30.
2. *The Living of These Days* (New York: Harper and Brothers, 1956), p. 92.
3. Ibid., p. 94.
4. Ibid., p. 98.
5. Ibid., p. 97.
6. Ibid., p. 99.
7. Ibid.
8. Clyde E. Fant and William M. Pinson, eds., *Twenty Centuries of Great Preaching*, vol. 9 (Waco, Tex.: Word Books, 1971), p. 17.
9. "The Great Hours of a Man's Life," in Harry Emerson Fosdick, *Riverside Sermons* (New York: Harper and Brothers, 1958), pp. 11-12.
10. "On Catching the Wrong Bus," in *Riverside Sermons*, p. 38.

CHAPTER 19: JAMES S. STEWART (1896–1990): PRESBYTERIAN—THE AUTHORITY OF EVANGELICAL TRADITION

1. *A Faith to Proclaim* (London: Hodder and Stoughton, 1953), p. 31.
2. *Heralds of God* (New York: Charles Scribner's Sons, 1946), p. 31.
3. Ibid., p. 61.
4. Ibid., pp. 62ff., 89.
5. Ibid., p. 84.
6. Ibid., pp. 79ff.
7. Ibid., p. 69.
8. Ibid., p. 109.
9. Ibid., p. 155.
10. Ibid., pp. 109ff.
11. Ibid., p. 154.
12. Ibid., pp. 123-40.
13. "The Wind of the Spirit," in *The Wind of the Spirit* (London: Hodder and Stoughton, 1968), pp. 9-10.
14. "Clouds and Darkness and the Morning Star," in *The Gates of New Life* (New York: Charles Scribner's Sons, 1940), p. 154.
15. *Heralds of God*, p. 92.

CHAPTER 20: MARTIN LUTHER KING, JR. (1929–1968): BLACK BAPTIST—THE AUTHORITY OF THE OPPRESSED

1. Quoted by David L. Lewis in "Martin Luther King, Jr.," *Encyclopaedia Britannica*, 1980.

2. James E. Massey, *Designing the Sermon* (Nashville: Abingdon, 1980); Henry H. Mitchell, *Black Preaching* (Nashville: Abingdon Press, 1990), *Celebration and Experience in Preaching* (Nashville: Abingdon Press, 1990); Bruce Rosenberg, *The Art of the American Folk-Preacher* (New York: Oxford University Press, 1970); and Richard Lischer, "The Word That Moves: The Preaching of Martin Luther King, Jr.," *Theology Today* 46 (July 1989): 169-82.

3. Lischer, "The Word That Moves," 172.

4. Ibid., 173.

5. Ibid., 180.

6. Ibid., 174.

7. Martin Luther King, Jr., *Conscience for Change: Massey Lectures, Seventh Series* (Toronto: Canadian Broadcasting Corporation, 1967), pp. 45-46.